Skip the Borders
Easy Patterns for Modern Quilts

JULIE HERMAN
of JAYBIRD QUILTS

Martingale®
Create with Confidence

Mission Statement

Dedicated to providing quality products
and service to inspire creativity.

Skip the Borders: Easy Patterns for Modern Quilts
© 2012 by Julie Herman

Martingale®
19021 120th Ave. NE, Ste. 102
Bothell, WA 98011-9511 USA
ShopMartingale.com

Printed in China
17 16 15 14 13 12   8 7 6 5 4 3 2 1

**Library of Congress Cataloging-in-Publication Data is
available upon request.**

ISBN: 978-1-60468-081-2

Credits

PRESIDENT & CEO: Tom Wierzbicki
EDITOR IN CHIEF: Mary V. Green
DESIGN DIRECTOR: Paula Schlosser
MANAGING EDITOR: Karen Costello Soltys
TECHNICAL EDITOR: Nancy Mahoney
COPY EDITOR: Sheila Chapman Ryan
PRODUCTION MANAGER: Regina Girard
ILLUSTRATOR: Robin Strobel
COVER & TEXT DESIGNER: Adrienne Smitke
PHOTOGRAPHER: Brent Kane

Dedication

I've always found dedications to be intriguing. People often say, "I couldn't have done this without you" and such. I guess for me it's more of, "I *wouldn't* have done this without you."

- My Grandpop Nate: My grandfather passed away in March 2009, and that event set me on the road to where I am today. My grandfather was the type of man that if he wanted to do something, he did it. He lived to be 92 and had an amazing life full of accomplishments. After he passed, I stopped saying, "one day..." and started saying, "today." I started my blog not long after.

- My brother, Brad: He's the one person I know who never immediately responds with a "no" or "that can't be done." While his thoughts often run into crazy tangents, he's the one person who has believed in every single idea I've ever come up with, no matter how wild.

- My dad: He's the practical one—the one that keeps our family grounded and who doesn't let things sit. He stays on top of things to make it all happen.

- My mom: She's the creative one who's always there at the 11th hour to sew on a binding, test a pattern, read my instructions, and give honest, real-time feedback.

I'm incredibly lucky to have such a supportive family and I *wouldn't* have done this without you.

Contents

Introduction

My goal in this book is to provide inspiring patterns. With the blueprint of a borderless quilt, you can expand your skills and create beautiful, one-of-a-kind quilts.

The thought of writing a book was always a scary and foreign one for me. I love to design, but writing? Hey, English was never my best subject. When I started my blog, I used to type in all lowercase letters! Writing this book has been an amazing experience for me—it's pushed me out of my comfort zone. I like to teach, so I drew on that to figure out the best way to put all the words together to teach through the printed page.

Believe it or not, I wrote most of this book on my iPad. I was working on my manuscript during a cross-country move to California, and I would take advantage of every opportunity to jot down a few words. In the end, I think writing the book as a stream of thoughts in small notes, rather than in the formal formatting of a large manuscript, was the reason I successfully got over my writer's block.

My path to quilting was one of self-discovery, with a lot of initial trial and error. Despite using terrible construction techniques on my first few quilts, I fell in love with the process and never looked back. Designing a quilt, playing with fabric and color, and then sewing the fabric pieces together became my outlet and my joy. Quilting is my place, where I feel like I can be exactly who I am. I hope quilting has done or will do the same for you.

Why Skip the Borders?

I've always compared borders on quilts to frames on photos or paintings. But who says you have to frame everything? Sometimes artwork stands better on its own. Sometimes a frame can just serve as a distraction. Think of canvas oil paintings—many start out as canvas stretched over stretcher bars, and that's just how they remain. They never get a frame or multiple mats. And they stand strongly on their own.

Which isn't to say frames are never necessary. They can give weight to the art and finish it off. The same goes for quilts. Borders can finish off a quilt and add impact. But many of us put borders on a quilt simply because we think we're supposed to. Often we make a table runner without a border, but not a larger quilt. Why is that?

Yes, borders are an easy way to make a quilt bigger, but what if a design is better without a border or frame? What if adding a border would just be a distraction?

Borderless quilts are not new, but they have enjoyed a resurgence within the last few years. Initially I created borderless quilts out of a personal desire to not cut and sew borders. Quickly I realized that some designs *needed* borders to feel complete. That idea led me on a journey of discovering how to eliminate the frame and still have a quilt design that was strong enough to stand alone.

Once I got to thinking about all of this, I started to sketch ideas for quilts without borders. In the beginning it felt like coloring outside the lines, but I quickly realized that it was more like coloring *in* the lines— but just having fewer lines. Taking away the borders meant that the quilt needed to have a strong structure and be able to support itself and stand alone. Many sketches just didn't work for one reason or another— often because the design of the blocks gives the impression of a lot of movement. Think of a complex quilt made from spinning Pinwheel blocks. A quilt like that needs a border to help visually contain all that's going on in the design.

Whether you're already pushing the limits, or this book is your attempt at breaking out of what you know, or you haven't made a single quilt yet, I hope you will learn something or try something new. Keep learning, keep growing, and join me on this borderless quilt journey!

Permission to Break the Rules

As a kid, I generally followed the rules without question; although I was sometimes curious, I didn't push boundaries too much. When I did break the rules it was usually with good reason. I would learn the "rule" first, and then figure out why it existed. I was never one to break a rule "just because."

The same can be said when I look at my approach to quiltmaking. Despite my backward entrance into this creative thing called quilting, I've found that I have the most success breaking a rule once I have a firm understanding of *why* the rule exists. Knowing the purpose can be a guide to knowing when, how, and why you want to skip that purpose.

All that being said, I'm a big believer in *no* quilt police. Quiltmaking is supposed to be fun. If you aren't having fun, then what's the point? So press your seam allowances open or press them to the side. Use bias binding or straight of grain. Do what works best for you!

Don't Underestimate the Binding

One aspect of a borderless quilt that becomes very important is your binding choice. You have lots of options when it comes to binding, and I'll cover these in greater detail later. But without a border to contain all of the elements in the quilt, the binding handles that job. Whether it's plain or striped, one color or scrappy, the binding is an important design element of a borderless quilt. Be sure to have a look at "Binding" on page 17 for ideas.

Structure of a Borderless Quilt

Quilts without borders need a strong pattern, or structure, to hold the design together since they don't have a unifying fabric around the perimeter of the quilt to do the job. This can be achieved through block design and block arrangement. While some quilts with borders have structure, not all do, and the design structure is often not essential since the border helps hold the quilt design together.

Early in the design process I was focused on structure. My goal was to determine what worked and what didn't work. Many star designs, for example, or blocks with strong diagonals didn't seem to work as well without borders. Often these designs need a border to feel complete.

Examples of Borderless Quilts

The first successful borderless star design I created was "Stars and Stripes" on page 55. The success in this design comes from the large blocks and careful color placement. The high-contrast background makes the stars the focus without needing to add borders. Not long after, I designed "White Stars," below and on page 27. I enjoy playing with positive and negative space, and this quilt was a result of experimenting with negative space.

Placing highly saturated colors in the position that's usually considered background gives the design a new life in "White Stars."

Blocks that have their own border tend to create fantastic borderless designs. Examples of this technique are "Floating Triangles" on the next page and page 37, "Square City" on page 51, "Box of Chocolates" on page 59, and "Framed Coins" below and on page 69. The structure in each block holds the entire quilt together. That being said, some of the quilts were too heavy or too boring with just one block.

In "Square City," I combined a pieced block with a plain block. Not only did this make the quilt more interesting, but it gives you the opportunity to feature large-scale prints throughout the quilt. On the other hand, "Framed Coins," didn't need the addition of another block, but a creative block layout was the perfect touch.

Notice how the blocks are oriented both horizontally and vertically in "Framed Coins."

Most of the quilts in this book seem to end at their edges, but a few have designs that could go on and on. This is achieved with an on-point setting where the blocks along the edges are chopped in half. "Boxed In" on page 45, "Raspberry Dessert" opposite and on page 61, and "In Between" on page 73 are great examples of this idea. It's almost as if you're seeing a snapshot of one section of an overall design that continues beyond the edges of the quilt. The on-point layout supports the abrupt ending by allowing your eye to continue moving around the quilt and, at the same time, creates a beautiful design.

If you're unsure about your color choices, try making a sample block and photographing it. Then use photo-editing software to play with the colors, change the quilt to gray scale, or even invert the colors to see other options. This process can help confirm your color selection or reveal that it's not the best choice, saving you from making blocks that you won't be in love with.

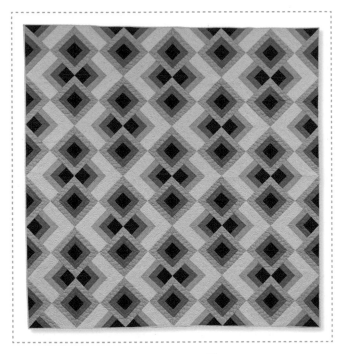

You could add a border to on-point designs to "hold them in," but it isn't necessary, as shown here in "Raspberry Dessert."

Color selection and placement is the last key component in structure. Some designs like "White Stars" (opposite and on page 27) and "Floating Triangles" (at right and on page 37) rely on high contrast. Other designs like "Chubby Logs" on page 33 and "Dot Dot Dash" at right and on page 43 are better suited for a scrappy array of fabrics that blend together, because the design doesn't require high contrast from one fabric to the next. In "Dot Dot Dash," the contrast of vertical lines and horizontal lines gives strength to the design. If too many high-contrast fabrics are used (instead of fabrics that blend together), the design would become secondary to the fabric placement. The result of using fabrics that blend in "Chubby Logs" is that the edges of each block seem to blur together and create one overall design. If high-contrast fabrics were used, this blurring wouldn't occur, and your eye would focus on one part of the block or the break between blocks rather than the quilt as a whole.

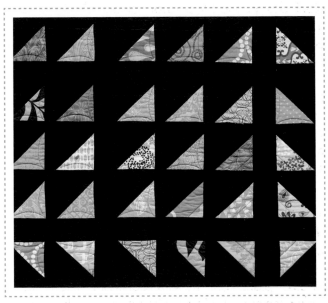

The sashing around the triangle-blocks in "Floating Triangles" creates the illusion that the blocks are floating.

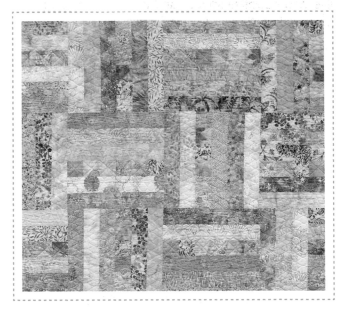

The batik fabrics used in "Dot Dot Dash" support the design without overwhelming it.

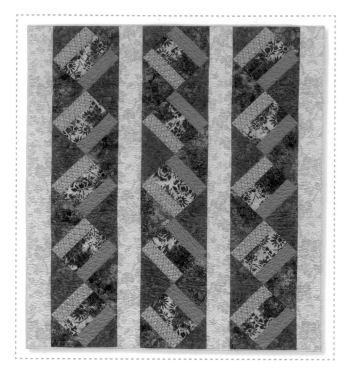

"In Between", page 73.

Keep in mind, with quilt design as with everything else, all things are relative. Some people will think "In Between" above is not borderless because vertical sashing is added to the outer-right and -left sides. Don't forget, I've given you permission to break the rules! Make what you want, how you want it, because it makes you happy. Heck, you can even add a border to one of these quilts if you really want to.

Quilt Categories

The quilts in this book are divided into three sections: "One-Block Quilts," "Two-Block Quilts," and "Outside-the-Block Quilts."

ONE-BLOCK QUILTS

All of the one-block quilts utilize one individual quilt block that's repeated throughout the design. Most blocks are square; however, "In Formation" shows that this concept can work with a rectangular block as well. Many one-block quilt designs take advantage of block rotation to give the illusion that the quilt is more complex than it really is. "Boxed In" uses color placement to give additional interest and create the feeling that there's more than one block.

"In Formation," page 39

"Boxed In," page 45

TWO-BLOCK QUILTS

Each two-block quilt takes advantage of using two different blocks to create the design. Two of the designs feature a pieced block alternated with a plain block, while two other designs feature two different pieced blocks. Using a second block adds another design element that can support the design structure. "Stars and Stripes" has mostly pieced blocks with a few plain blocks thrown in for balance. The two different pieced blocks in "Raspberry Dessert" combine to appear as one larger block.

OUTSIDE-THE-BLOCK QUILTS

Last, but not least, are the outside-the-block quilts. These quilts include designs that are based on row quilts (both horizontal and vertical), non-square units, and quilts in which a recognizable block doesn't exist at all. For these designs I found that simple is best. When I tried using a detailed block with this type of quilt layout, it always felt as if something were missing.

"Rows of Bricks," page 67

"Stars and Stripes," page 55

"Checkerboard Dots," page 77

"Raspberry Dessert," page 61

Basic Quiltmaking Instructions

On the pages that follow, you'll find valuable information to help you with the successful completion of your quilt.

Fabric Basics

I used 100% cotton fabrics to make all of the quilts in this book. Most of the fabric requirements are based on 42"-wide fabrics. A little extra yardage has been included to allow for shrinkage and errors in cutting, but if the fabric is a "must-have," I always suggest buying extra!

TO PREWASH OR NOT TO PREWASH?

This question has been asked over and over and there's a benefit to both. Years ago the dyes used in fabrics were not nearly as colorfast as they are today, so prewashing was a must. Modern dyes, along with the use of fewer chemicals in the fabric-making process, have made prewashing a personal choice.

Prewashing is not advised when working with precut fabric bundles. Washing will distort the precut fabrics and defeat the convenience of the product. Keep in mind that all additional fabrics, such as backgrounds, binding, and backing, should also *not* be prewashed when combined with precuts. All the fabrics in one project should be handled the same way. If you don't prewash, consider using a dye-attracting laundry sheet in the washing machine the first time you launder the quilt.

Prewashing is advised when working with deeply saturated colors such as navy or red. It's also best to prewash hand-dyed or batik fabrics. Fabrics will shrink a bit when prewashed, so purchasing a little extra is always recommended. Personally, I don't prewash my fabric unless I absolutely need to. I prefer sewing with unwashed fabric—and saving time.

Solids or Prints?

How about both! Some quilts in this book feature only print fabrics, such as "Four-Patch Shift" on page 29, "Chubby Logs" on page 33, "Square City" on page 51, and "Box of Chocolates" at right and on page 59. Then, there's "In Formation" above right and on page 39, which features only solid fabrics. "White Stars" below and on page 27, "Stars and Stripes" on page 55 and "Framed Coins" on page 69, show how prints and solids can work together.

So how do you know what's best? I let the project speak to me.

"In Formation" felt like it needed a gradation of solids to best show off the design, and adding prints would distract from the sharp angles in the design.

"White Stars" needed the contrast of fun, bright, busy prints in the background to make the stars pop.

"Box of Chocolates" has many prints that read as almost solids, but adding in actual solids would have disrupted the flow of the design.

Rotary Cutting

Rotary cutting is a fast and accurate way to cut the pieces you need to make a quilt. I strongly suggest that you use the same brand of rulers for cutting all the pieces of a project. Each company produces its rulers differently, which can create small size differences between different brands. These small differences can add up and cause you problems down the road.

I used a special ruler to make "Stars and Stripes" on page 55 and "Box of Chocolates" on page 59. For those projects, I recommend using a 90° Double-Strip Ruler by Creative Grids. This ruler allows you to accurately cut multiple 90° triangles from a strip set, saving time and minimizing fabric waste.

The cutting instructions for each project list how many strips to cut and how to crosscut those strips. All rotary-cutting instructions include a standard ¼"-wide seam allowance. If you're unfamiliar with rotary cutting, follow these basic rotary-cutting instructions.

1. Fold your fabric in half and match the selvages. Place the fabric on your cutting mat with the folded edge closest to you. Align a square ruler along the left side of the folded edge. Place a 6" x 24" ruler to the left of the square ruler, just covering the uneven raw edges on the left side of the fabric. Remove the square ruler and cut along the right edge of the long ruler to create a straight edge. Discard this strip. (Reverse this procedure if you are left-handed.)

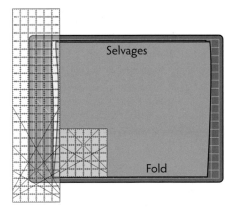

2. To cut strips, align the newly cut edge of the fabric with the ruler markings at the required width. For example, to cut a 3"-wide strip, place the 3" ruler mark on the edge of the fabric. Carefully cut along the right edge of the ruler.

3. To cut squares and rectangles, cut the strips the required width. Trim the selvage ends of the strips. Align the desired measurement on the ruler with the left edge of the strip and cut a square or rectangle. If cutting multiple same-sized pieces, you can keep the strip folded in half and cut two pieces at the same time.

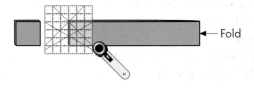

4. Some projects require you to cut triangles. To do this, cut squares as described in step 3. Then, following the project instructions, cut the square in half diagonally to make half-square triangles or into quarters diagonally to make quarter-square triangles. Handle the triangles carefully; the sides are cut on the bias and can stretch out of shape.

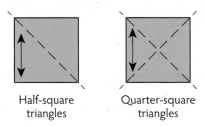

Half-square triangles   Quarter-square triangles

Machine Piecing

The key to successful machine piecing is sewing with an accurate ¼"-wide seam allowance. Using a ¼" presser foot can help this process.

Strip piecing. Many projects in this book take advantage of strip piecing to save time. This process involves sewing two or more long strips together to make a strip set. Press the seam allowances open. Then square up one end of the strip set and crosscut it into the desired segments or units.

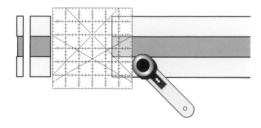

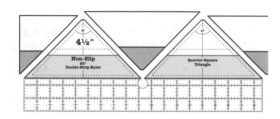

Chain piecing. This is another timesaving technique. You could sew one unit, cut your thread, and then press the unit. Or you could sew multiple pieces at once and save a lot of time. Cut all of the pieces required. Place piles of the pieces next to your sewing machine, arranging them in the order they will be sewn. Feed the pieces under your presser foot, one after another, without stopping to cut the threads. After all of the units are sewn, cut the chain to remove the units from the machine and clip the threads between the units. Then press the units as directed.

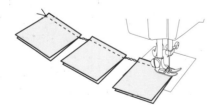

Pressing

Pressing is essential to creating an accurate and flat quilt top. Pressing is not the same as ironing. To press, place the iron on top of the piece and press without moving the iron back and forth across the piece. Moving the iron along the pieces or unit can cause distortion.

Just like the "To Prewash or Not to Prewash?" discussion on page 12, there is a debate about pressing. Some say to press the seam allowances to one side, while others say to press them open. When I started quilting, I pressed the seam allowances to one side because I was told it was the only way. The more time I spend sewing, the more I realize that each project is different and many times pressing the seam allowances open will reduce bulk and create a flatter seam with more accurate results. Throughout the book I tell you to press the seam allowances open. But have no fear, if you're a press-to-the-side kind of person—that's A-OK too!

Pinning

A word about pinning: When seam allowances are pressed open, you won't be able to abut opposing seam allowances. I've found I don't need to use pins very often, but when I do, I simply align the seam lines, matching any seam intersections, and pin them in place.

Assembling the Quilt Top

After finishing all of the blocks, it's time to assemble the quilt top! Use a large square ruler to double check that all the blocks are the same size. If any blocks are too large or too small, take the time now to remake them. You can ease a ⅛" difference along a block side, but not much more than that without making a bumpy quilt top.

Arrange the blocks as shown in the quilt diagram. It can be helpful to use a design wall for this step. Using a design wall gives you the opportunity to rearrange blocks and ensure balance in the color and scale of your arrangement.

Sew the blocks together as directed in the pattern. Use as many pins as you feel necessary to ensure that points and seam intersections match. Trim excess loose threads along the way.

Borderless quilts have many more exposed seams around the outer edges than quilts with borders. It's helpful to baste any seam intersections about ⅛" from the outer edges to stabilize the seams and ensure that they don't unravel before quilting.

Quilt Backs

I like to make the back of a quilt just as fun as the front. Do you think about the back of your quilt? Do you buy extra fabric at the start for the back? Or wait till you are done to think about it? The back of a quilt can be a forgotten space, but it doesn't have to be! You can make a simple quilt back from one fabric or you can get creative. I've done a variety of things with the backs of my quilts.

One thing I do these days is to piece my label into the backing. Unfortunately, quilts get lost or even stolen. Thieves will remove the label if possible to hide the creator's identity. By piecing the label into the backing and quilting over the label, it's impossible to remove the label without making a hole in the back of the quilt.

Keep in mind whether you'll be quilting your quilt or sending it to be professionally machine quilted. The backing should be at least 4" to 6" larger than the quilt top (2" to 3" on all sides). However, a long-arm quilter needs extra fabric around the sides so that the edges of the quilt are far enough away from the roller bars; therefore you should check with the quilter before you prepare your backing. Be sure to place your label away from the edges, otherwise the label may accidentally get cut off.

You can make a simple backing from one fabric. For the quilts in this book, I've listed enough backing fabric to piece the backing with one seam. Most of the backings are pieced with a horizontal seam, since this is the best use of the fabric. If you prefer a vertical seam, you'll need to purchase additional fabric.

To make a simple quilt back, remove the selvages and piece the backing pieces together with ½"-wide seam allowances. Press the seam allowances open.

To make a quilt back that incorporates a label, like the ones shown on page 16, follow these steps. The label strip can be placed horizontally, as described below, or vertically.

1. Make a printed, handwritten, or embroidered label. Then add a fabric frame around the label. The frame can be the same width on all sides, or not. It can be from one fabric or pieces left over from making the quilt top.
2. Pin the quilt top to a design wall so that you can easily see how large it is. If you don't have a design wall, lay the quilt on your floor or a large table.

3. For the top part of the backing, select a piece of fabric that's at least 6" wider than the quilt top by the full width of the fabric. For instance, if the quilt top is 50" wide the fabric would need to be at least 56" x 42". Pin this piece of fabric on top of the quilt top with 2" or 3" extending beyond the top edge.

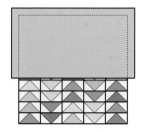

4. For the bottom of the backing, select a second piece of fabric that's the same size as or larger than the first fabric piece. Cut the second fabric to the same width as the first fabric. Pin the second fabric to the design wall, covering the quilt top, and leaving a space for the label strip.

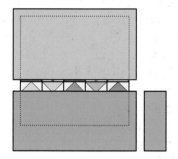

5. Measure the height of the framed label from step 1 and cut two pieces of fabric the same height. Sew them to either side of the label to create the label strip. The label can be centered or off center; just make sure the label is at least 6" to 8" from the outer edge of the quilt top and that the label strip is wider than the fabric pieces in step 4. Once you've decided where to place the label, trim the label strip to the same width as the other two fabric pieces.

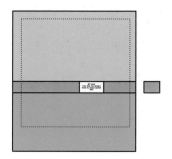

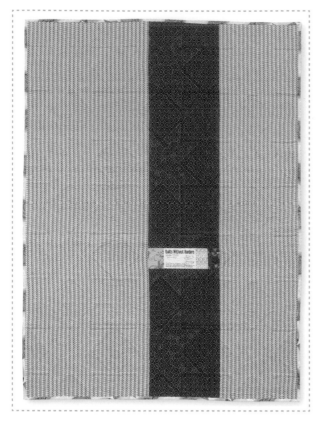

The label on the back of "White Stars" is pieced with a high-contrast strip and joined to the two backing pieces with a vertical seam.

A scrappy label is pieced into a horizontal strip on the back of "Rows of Bricks."

6. Remove the selvages from the top and bottom fabrics and make sure that each fabric has a nice straight edge. Sew the backing fabrics to each long side of the label strip using a ½"-wide seam allowance. On the bottom fabric, trim away the excess, leaving at least 3" beyond the edge of the quilt top. Or you can wait and trim the excess after the quilting is completed. If you plan to have the quilt professionally machine quilted, check with the long-arm quilter before trimming.

Preparing to Quilt

Once you've finished your quilt top and pieced your backing, you're almost done. At this point you'll need to decide if you're going to quilt your quilt, or if you're going to send it to a professional long-arm quilter. If you plan to have your quilt professionally machine quilted, the quilt doesn't need to be layered and basted. If you plan to machine quilt using your home sewing machine, follow these instructions to sandwich the layers together.

1. Lay the backing, wrong side up, on a flat, clean surface (use a table for small quilts and the floor for large quilts). Anchor the backing to the flat surface with blue painter's tape; the backing should be taut, but not stretched out of shape.
2. Center the batting over the backing, smoothing out any wrinkles.
3. Center the quilt top, right side up, over the batting, smoothing out any wrinkles. You should have excess batting and backing all around the top.
4. For machine quilting, place safety pins 3" to 4" apart to hold the three layers together.
5. I usually send my quilts to be machine quilted by a long-arm professional, but if you want guidance in quilting your projects, there are many good books and magazines available where you can find instructions for quilting designs.

Binding

Binding is the last step in completing a quilt and encases the raw edges of the quilt top, backing, and batting. But when it comes to borderless quilts, binding is not *just* about finishing the quilt.

Binding is often overlooked as an opportunity to make a final statement with fabric selection. Depending on the design, you may want the binding to stand out or fade into the quilt. In this section, you'll learn about some of the choices you have. I'll explain the ins and outs of each choice so that you can pick the one that works best for you.

Straight-of-Grain or Bias Binding?

I'm asked this question very often. Through my years of working at a quilt shop, taking classes, and reading many books, I've learned the differences between straight-of-grain and bias binding. Straight-of-grain binding is cut along the grain of the fabric, usually across the width of the fabric. Bias binding is cut on the bias, at a 45° angle to the grain of the fabric.

The main reason to use bias binding over straight-of-grain binding is strength. The woven threads in a bias binding wrap diagonally around the quilt so the wear is spread out more than with straight-of-grain binding.

The table below shows the pros and cons of straight-of-grain versus bias binding. I use both types of binding and let the project determine which is best. Keep in mind, the design printed on a binding fabric may dictate which type of binding is best.

Here are my personal recommendations: Use straight-of-grain binding for wall quilts and decorative items that won't get a lot of use. Use bias binding for bed quilts and lap quilts, as well as anything you plan on washing frequently.

Straight-of-grain binding using a tone-on-tone fabric

Bias binding using a solid fabric

STRAIGHT-OF-GRAIN	BIAS
Easy to cut	Time consuming to cut
Limited waste	More waste if you don't plan well
Less strength; doesn't wear as well	Stronger, more durable
Less stretch or give; suitable for binding straight edges only	More stretch or give; perfect for binding curves

What about Color?

The color and print (or lack of print) you use for your binding fabric can change the look of the entire project. Do you want your binding to pop and stand out? Or do you want it to blend into the quilt and look like it isn't even there? Especially when working with a borderless design, choosing an appropriate binding fabric is a key decision to make. I suggest auditioning binding options to get a feel for what will work best. Sometimes it can even help to take a few photos and wait a day or two to decide. Below are a few of the color options you can consider.

Variety of striped bindings

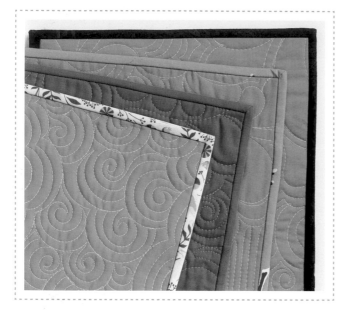

Bindings can be a similar color to the backing or a contrasting color.

Scrappy Binding

Another great choice is a scrappy binding, which can be achieved in several ways. One way is to use leftover binding strips from other projects. Piece them together until you have the length you need.

Another way is to create a pieced unit from straight-of-grain strips. Sew the strips together along their long edges to make a rectangle, and then cut this strip-pieced rectangle into bias binding strips.

Stripes

In general, my number one go-to binding-fabric choice is a stripe. I look for a stripe that coordinates with my project and cut it on the bias for a diagonal-striped look. You can use stripes that run either the width or the length of the fabric. If the stripe is printed diagonally on the fabric, cut strips straight across the width of the fabric to have the same diagonal effect. And of course, stripes can also be cut on the straight of grain for a different look.

Scrappy bias binding

Adding a Binding Flange

A binding flange is a folded strip of fabric that rests between the binding and the quilt front. Flanges are great when you need a tiny pop of color before the binding. They can also be used to separate busy fabrics used in blocks from a busy binding. Depending on the color, a flange can create contrast between the binding and the quilt, or help them to blend together. A flange also can create the illusion of a mini border.

Flanges are simple to make and are added to the quilt edges after the quilting is completed and before attaching the binding. Note: I don't suggest using a flange when a quilt design has points that go to the outer edge; the flange will cover the points.

Wide and narrow flanges

To make a binding flange, follow these instructions.

1. Cut enough strips from the flange fabric to go around the outside of the quilt. For a narrow 1/8"-wide flange, cut the strips 3/4" wide. For a wider 1/4"-wide flange, cut the strips 1" wide.
2. Sew the strips together end to end with diagonal seams. Trim the excess fabric and press the seam allowances open.

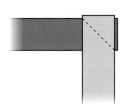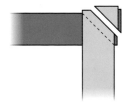

3. Press the strip in half lengthwise, wrong sides together and with the raw edges aligned.

4. Measure the length of the quilt and cut two strips to fit that measurement. Pin the flange to the sides of the quilt, matching the raw edges of the flange with the quilt edges. Use a long stitch length, a walking foot, and a 1/8"-wide seam allowance to baste the strips to the quilt.

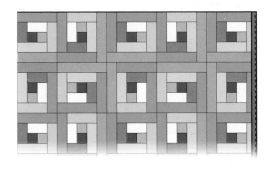

5. Measure the width of the quilt and cut two strips to fit that measurement. Baste the strips to the top and bottom edges of the quilt top, overlapping the strips in the corners.

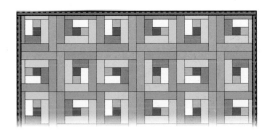

6. Apply the binding on top of the flange. Remember to set the stitch length on your machine back to its normal length so your binding isn't basted to the quilt!

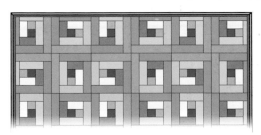

Binding-Width Options

I usually cut 2¼"-wide binding strips. Many patterns and books list 2½"-wide strips as the standard measurement. The main difference is a visual one—with wider binding strips, more binding will show on the back of the quilt.

- 2"-wide binding stitched with a ¼"-wide seam allowance will appear the same on the front and back. When the binding is turned to the back, it can be difficult for the folded edge to cover the row of machine stitching because the binding is narrow. (White-print binding shown below.)
- 2¼"-wide binding stitched with a ¼"-wide seam allowance will have slightly more binding showing on the back of the quilt; it's easier to hand sew in place than a narrower binding. (Tan binding shown below.)
- 2½"-wide binding stitched with a ¼"-wide seam allowance will have even more binding showing on the back of the quilt. (Dark-purple binding shown below.)

Backs of quilts showing the different binding widths

How Much Binding Is Needed?

Unless you're making a tiny quilt, you'll need to join multiple strips to make a binding strip long enough to go around the perimeter of your quilt. All of the quilt instructions in this book list how much binding is needed. However, if you want to use a different technique or width of binding strips, use the basic information provided here to determine how much fabric is required.

To calculate how much binding you'll need, simply measure the perimeter of the quilt and add 10" extra for seam allowances and turning the corners. For instance, if the quilt measures 42" x 64", add 42 + 42 + 64 + 64 = 212; 212 + 10 = 222. You'll need 222" of binding. This tells you how many *inches* of binding you need. Depending on whether you're using straight-of-grain or bias binding, the yardage amount required and the cutting is different, but the total number of inches needed remains the same.

STRAIGHT-OF-GRAIN BINDING

If you're making straight-of-grain binding, divide the number of inches needed by the usable width of your binding fabric. In general, I use 40" to account for seam allowances and err on the side of cutting more strips rather than not having enough. In this example, 222 ÷ 40 = 5.55. Round that up to the next whole number, and you'll discover you need to cut six binding strips for your quilt.

BIAS BINDING

Calculating the yardage required for bias binding involves using the square-root button on your calculator. But for a quick reference you can put away your calculator and use the following chart as a guide for 2¼"-wide binding. The chart lists how many inches of bias binding you can cut from a square.

SIZE OF SQUARE	INCHES OF BINDING
20"	175"
21"	195"
22"	215"
23"	235"
24"	250"
25"	275"
26"	300"
27"	320"
28"	345"
29"	370"
30"	395"
36"	570"
40"	700"

Cutting Bias Strips

Using a rotary cutter is a fast and easy way to cut bias strips, but can yield some waste. This method works very well when you want to make a lot of binding from the same fabric.

1. Refer to "How Much Binding Is Needed?" on page 20 to determine how much binding you'll need for your quilt.
2. Trim off the selvages of the binding fabric. Fold one end of the fabric and align the trimmed, short edge with the long side of the fabric.

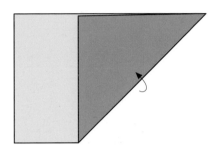

3. Place a 6" x 24" ruler on the fabric so that one of the crosswise lines is aligned with the fold. Cutting along the right edge of the ruler, cut off the corner triangle of fabric.

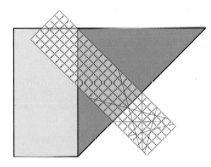

4. Move the ruler over so that the 2¼" line is aligned with the newly cut edge of the triangle. Cut along the edge of the ruler to make your first bias strip. Continue cutting 2¼"-wide strips. Utilize as much of the triangle as possible, but stop cutting strips as you approach the corner. Those strips will be very short and will add additional seams when making the binding.

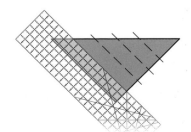

5. Carefully rotate the larger piece of fabric without disturbing the cut edges. Continue cutting 2¼"-wide strips until you have the required amount of binding strips.

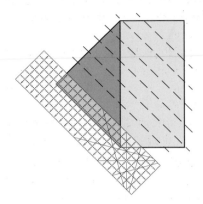

Joining Bias Strips

1. Place two binding strips right sides together with the diagonal edges aligned. Slide the strips so that the ends extend ¼" as shown. Sew across the cut edges using a ¼"-wide seam allowance.

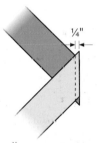

2. Press the seam allowances open and trim off any part of the seam allowance that extends beyond the edge of the binding.

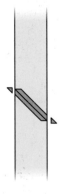

Press seam
allowances open.

3. Continue adding strips in the same manner until you have the required amount of binding.

Joining Straight-of-Grain Strips

1. Referring to "Rotary Cutting" on page 13, cut the required number of 2¼"-wide strips for the project you're making. With right sides together, overlap the strips at a 90° (right) angle. Stitch across the corner.
2. Trim the excess fabric, leaving a ¼" seam allowance. Press the seam allowances open.

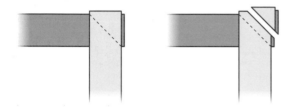

Attaching the Binding

1. Cut one end of the long binding strip at a 45° angle. Fold the binding in half lengthwise, wrong sides together, and press.

2. Beginning with the angled end of the binding strip, align the raw edge of the strip with the raw edges of the quilt. Starting on one side of the quilt (not at a corner) and beginning 8" from the strip's angled end, use a walking foot and a ¼"-wide seam allowance to stitch the binding strip to the quilt. Stop ¼" from the first corner and backstitch.

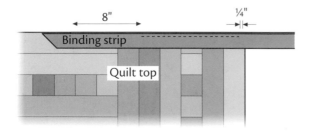

3. Remove the quilt from the sewing machine. Fold the binding up and away from the quilt so that the fold forms a 45° angle. Fold the binding back down onto itself, even with the edge of the quilt top. Pin the angled pleat in place. Begin with a backstitch at the fold of the binding and continue stitching along the edge of the quilt top, mitering each corner as you come to it.

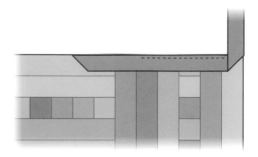

4. Stop sewing 12" from the starting (angled) end of the binding strip and backstitch. Remove the quilt from the machine. Place the quilt on a flat surface and open the ending tail. Open the beginning (angled) tail and overlap it on top of the ending tail as shown. Use a pencil to draw a line on the ending tail where it meets the beginning tail.

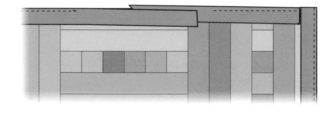

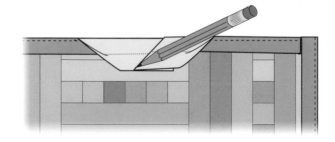

5. Fold the beginning tail out of the way and draw a second line ½" to the right of the first line. Make sure the second line is at a 45° angle and on the excess side of the ending tail.

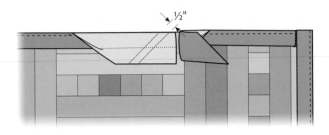

6. Cut the ending tail strip along the second line. The ends of both strips will form 45° angles and overlap ½".

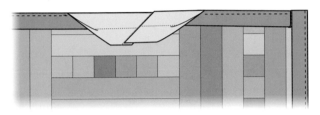

7. Place the binding ends right sides together, aligning the angled raw edges and being careful not to twist the strips. Pin in place. Fold the quilt out of the way and stitch the ends together using a ¼"-wide seam allowance.

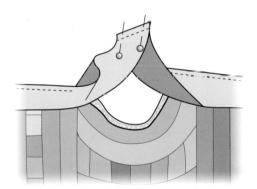

8. Press the seam allowances open, refold the binding, and press the fold. Then finish stitching the binding to the quilt.

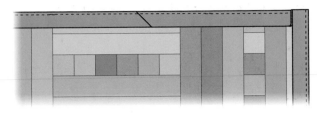

9. Fold the binding around to the back of the quilt and use binding clips to hold it in place. Using thread to match the binding, hand stitch the binding in place so that the folded edge covers the row of machine stitching. Neatly miter each corner.

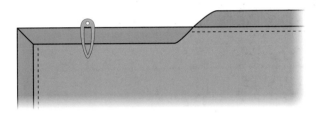

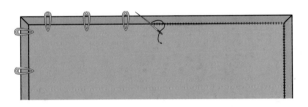

Making Scrappy Bias Binding

Scrappy bias binding can be made several ways. The scrappy binding on "Checkerboard Dots" on page 77 was made using the following method.

1. Cut six strips, 2½" x 42".
2. Sew the strips together along their long edges using a ¼"-wide seam allowance and offsetting the strips by approximately 2" to make a strip set. (Offsetting the strips will help avoid waste in the next step.) Press the seam allowances open.

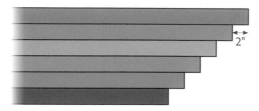

Offset strips approximately 2".

3. Position your ruler so that the 45° line is aligned with the seam line and trim the end of the strip set. If your ruler doesn't have a 45° line, you can use the marks on your cutting mat, although they aren't as accurate, especially if your mat has been used often.

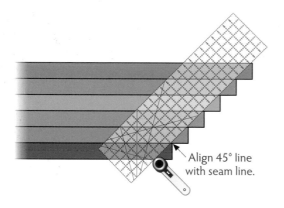

Align 45° line with seam line.

4. Turn the strip around, align the newly cut edge of the fabric with the ruler markings, and cut 2¼"-wide strips. Continue cutting strips until you have the desired number of inches for the binding.

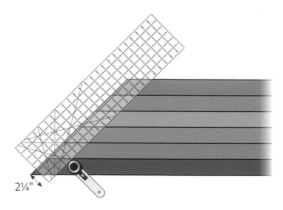

5. Join the bias strips using a ¼" seam allowance as described in "Joining Bias Strips" on page 21. Press the seam allowances open. Repeat to make one long, continuous strip.
6. Refer to "Attaching the Binding" on page 22 to stitch the scrappy binding to your quilt top.

ONE-BLOCK QUILTS

All of the one-block quilts are made using just one individual quilt block that's repeated. Read all of the directions before beginning; fabric placement is often key to making this type of quilt design work well.

Pieced by Julie Herman; machine quilted by Angela Walters

White Stars

FINISHED QUILT: 48½" x 64½" | FINISHED BLOCK: 16" x 16"

Materials

Yardage is based on 42"-wide fabric. Fat quarters measure 18" x 21".

2½ yards of white solid for stars
12 fat quarters of assorted prints for background
¾ yard of teal-and-white print for bias binding
3⅓ yards of fabric for backing
54" x 70" piece of batting

Cutting

From *each* of the 12 assorted fat quarters, cut:
4 rectangles, 4½" x 8½", using cutting diagram below (48 total)
4 squares, 4½" x 4½", using cutting diagram below (48 total)

From the white solid, cut:
3 strips, 8½" x 42"; crosscut into 12 squares, 8½" x 8½"
12 strips, 4½" x 42"; crosscut into 96 squares, 4½" x 4½"

From the teal-and-white print, cut:
240" of 2¼"-wide bias binding

Play with negative space to make this shining star quilt.

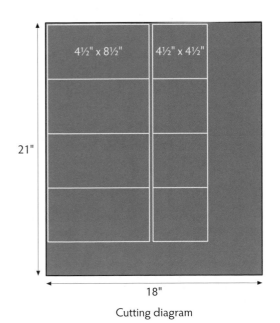

4½" x 8½"   4½" x 4½"

21"

18"

Cutting diagram

Making the Blocks

1. Draw a diagonal line on the wrong side of the 4½" white squares. Place a marked square on one end of an assorted rectangle, right sides together, and sew along the marked line as shown. Trim away the corner fabric, leaving a ¼" seam allowance. Press the seam allowances open.

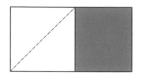

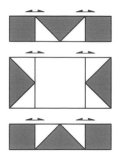

2. Place a second marked square on the opposite end of the rectangle, right sides together. Sew along the marked line and trim as before. Press the seam allowances open. Repeat steps 1 and 2 to make a total of 48 flying-geese units.

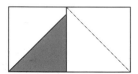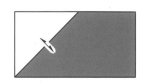

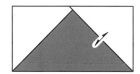

Make 48.

3. Arrange four matching flying-geese units, four assorted squares that match the flying-geese units, and one 8½" white square as shown.

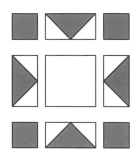

4. Sew the pieces together in rows; press the seam allowances open. Sew the rows together to complete the block. Press the seam allowances open. Repeat to make a total of 12 blocks.

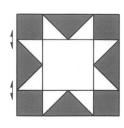

Make 12.

Quilt-Top Assembly

1. Referring to "Assembling the Quilt Top" on page 14, lay out the blocks in four rows of three blocks each.
2. Sew the blocks together in rows and press the seam allowances open. Sew the rows together; press.

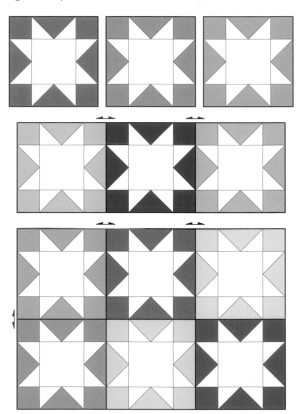

Finishing the Quilt

Refer to pages 15–24 for finishing your quilt, or take it to your favorite long-arm quilter for finishing. Using the 2¼"-wide bias binding strips, make and attach binding.

Four-Patch Shift

FINISHED QUILT: 54½" x 72½" | FINISHED BLOCK: 9" x 9"

Materials

Yardage is based on 42"-wide fabric.

⅔ yard of pale-yellow print for four-patch units
⅔ yard of purple print for four-patch units
⅜ yard *each* of 16 assorted prints for blocks
⅝ yard of pale-green print for binding
3⅝ yards of fabric for backing
60" x 78" piece of batting

Cutting

From the pale-yellow print, cut:
7 strips, 2¾" x 42"

From the purple print, cut:
7 strips, 2¾" x 42"

From *each* of the 16 assorted prints, cut:
2 strips, 5" x 42"; crosscut into:
    3 rectangles, 5" x 9½" (48 total)
    3 squares, 5" x 5" (48 total)

From the pale-green print, cut:
7 binding strips, 2¼" x 42"

This enticing quilt puts a new spin on the basic four-patch unit.

Making the Blocks

1. Sew a pale-yellow strip to the long side of a purple strip to make a strip set. Repeat to make a total of seven strip sets. Press the seam allowances open. Cut the strip sets into 96 segments, 2¾" wide.

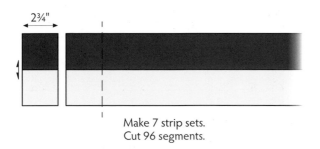

2¾"

Make 7 strip sets.
Cut 96 segments.

Pieced by Julie Herman; machine quilted by Angela Walters

2. Sew two segments from step 1 together to make a four-patch unit. Press the seam allowances open. Make a total of 48 units.

Make 48.

3. Sew a four-patch unit to an assorted print square, making sure to orient the colors in the four-patch *exactly* as shown. Press the seam allowances open.

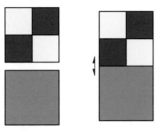

Make 48.

4. Sew a matching rectangle to the bottom of the unit from step 3 to complete the block. Press the seam allowances open. Repeat to make a total of 48 blocks.

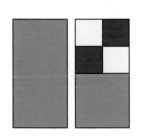

Make 48.

Quilt-Top Assembly

1. Referring to "Assembling the Quilt Top" on page 14, lay out the blocks in eight rows of six blocks each. In the odd-numbered rows, rotate the blocks so that the four-patch units are in the top-right and bottom-right corners. In the even-numbered rows, rotate the blocks so that the four-patch units are in the top-left and bottom-left corners.

2. Sew the blocks together in rows, pressing the seam allowances open. Sew the rows together and press.

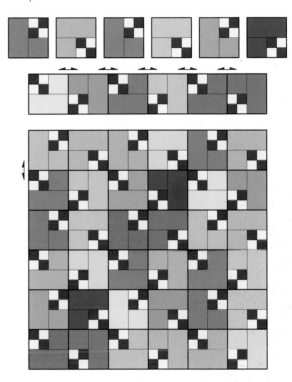

Finishing the Quilt

Refer to pages 15–24 for finishing your quilt, or take it to your favorite long-arm quilter for finishing. Using the 2¼"-wide pale-green binding strips, make and attach binding.

Pieced by Julie Herman; machine quilted by Angela Walters

Chubby Logs

FINISHED QUILT: 60½" x 60½" | FINISHED BLOCK: 10" x 10"

Materials

Yardage is based on 42"-wide fabric.

1 yard of gray floral #1 for blocks
1 yard of gray tone-on-tone print for blocks
   and binding
¾ yard of white-and-coral print for blocks
¾ yard of green-and-coral print for blocks
½ yard of pink-and-coral print for blocks
½ yard of gray floral #2 for blocks
½ yard of gray-and-tan print for blocks
½ yard of coral print for blocks and binding flange
⅓ yard of gray print for blocks
4⅛ yards of fabric for backing
66" x 66" piece of batting

Cutting

From the gray print, cut:
3 strips, 2½" x 42"

From the coral print, cut:
3 strips, 2½" x 42"
/ flange strips, 1" x 42"

From the gray-and-tan print, cut:
5 strips, 2½" x 42"; crosscut into 36 rectangles,
   2½" x 4½"

From the gray floral #2, cut:
5 strips, 2½" x 42"; crosscut into 36 rectangles,
   2½" x 4½"

From the gray tone-on-tone print, cut:
6 strips, 2½" x 42"; crosscut into 36 rectangles,
   2½" x 6½"
7 binding strips, 2¼" x 42"

From the pink-and-coral print, cut:
6 strips, 2½" x 42"; crosscut into 36 rectangles,
   2½" x 6½"

For this quilt, mix together large- and small-scale fabrics from two color families.

From the green-and-coral print, cut:
9 strips, 2½" x 42"; crosscut into 36 rectangles,
   2½" x 8½"

From the white-and-coral print, cut:
9 strips, 2½" x 42"; crosscut into 36 rectangles,
   2½" x 8½"

From the gray floral #1, cut:
12 strips, 2½" x 42"; crosscut into 36 rectangles,
   2½" x 10½"

Making the Blocks

1. Sew a 2½" gray strip to the long side of a 2½" coral strip to make a strip set. Press the seam allowances open. Repeat to make a total of three strip sets. Cut the strip sets into 36 segments, 2½" wide.

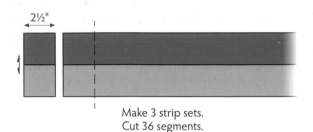

Make 3 strip sets.
Cut 36 segments.

2. Sew a gray-and-tan print rectangle to the right side of a unit from step 1. Press the seam allowances open.

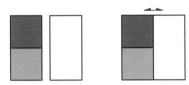

3. Sew a gray floral #2 rectangle to the top of the unit. Press the seam allowances open.

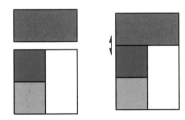

4. Sew a gray tone-on-tone rectangle to the left side of the unit. Press the seam allowances open.

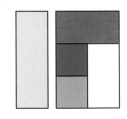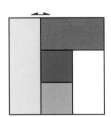

5. Sew a pink-and-coral rectangle to the bottom of the unit. Press the seam allowances open.

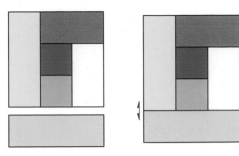

6. Sew a green-and-coral rectangle to the right side of the unit. Press the seam allowances open.

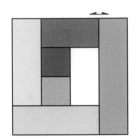

7. Sew a white-and-coral rectangle to the top of the unit. Press the seam allowances open.

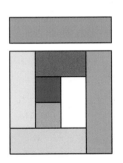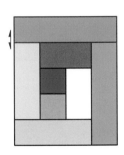

8. Sew a gray floral #1 rectangle to the left side of the unit. Press the seam allowances open. Repeat steps 2–8 to make a total of 36 blocks.

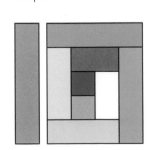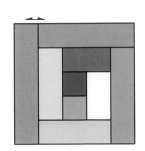

Make 36.

Quilt-Top Assembly

1. Referring to "Assembling the Quilt Top" on page 14, lay out four blocks with the gray large-scale floral in the center as shown. Sew the blocks together to create a large-block unit. Press the seam allowances open. Repeat to make a total of nine large-block units.

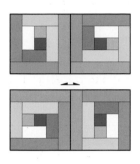
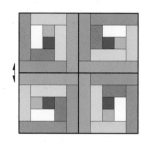

Make 9.

2. Lay out the large-block units in three rows of three units each as shown below. Sew the units together in rows, pressing the seam allowances open. Sew the rows together and press.

Finishing the Quilt

Refer to pages 15–24 for finishing your quilt, or take it to your favorite long-arm quilter for finishing. Using the 1"-wide coral strips, make and attach a binding flange. Using the 2¼"-wide gray tone-on-tone binding strips, make and attach binding.

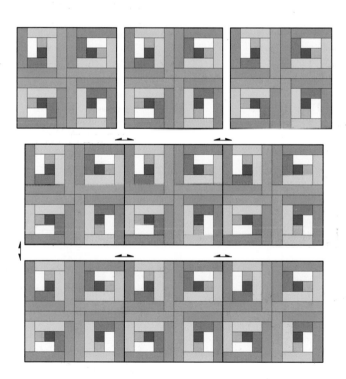

Pieced by Julie Herman; machine quilted by Angela Walters

Floating Triangles

FINISHED QUILT: 39½" x 39½" | FINISHED BLOCK: 13" x 13"

Materials

Yardage is based on 42"-wide fabric. Fat eighths measure 9" x 21".

2⅛ yards of brown tone-on-tone fabric for blocks and binding

27 fat eighths of assorted green and blue prints for blocks

2⅞ yards of fabric for backing

45" x 45" piece of batting

Cutting

From *each* of the 27 assorted green and blue prints, cut:

3 squares, 3½" x 3½" (81 total)

From the brown tone-on-tone fabric, cut:

6 strips, 1½" x 42"; crosscut into:
    9 rectangles, 1½" x 13½"
    9 rectangles, 1½" x 12½"

11 strips, 4½" x 42"; crosscut into 81 squares, 4½" x 4½"

5 binding strips, 2¼" x 42"

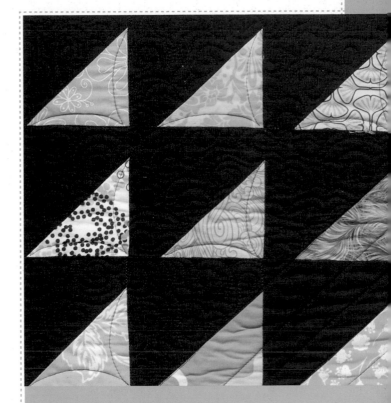

A simple quilt becomes a stunner when the blocks are set in an unusual way.

Making the Blocks

1. Draw a diagonal line from corner to corner on the wrong side of the blue and green squares. Place a marked square on one corner of a brown square, right sides together, and sew along the marked line as shown. Trim away the corner fabric, leaving a ¼" seam allowance. Press the seam allowances open. Repeat to make a total of 81 units.

Make 81.

2. Arrange nine units in three rows of three units each, as shown. Sew the units into rows; press the seam allowances open. Sew the rows together and press the seam allowances open. Make nine.

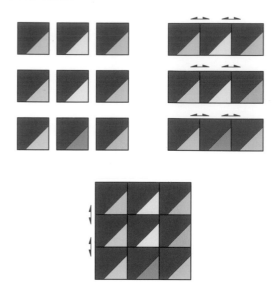

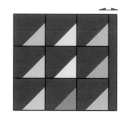

3. Sew a 1½" x 12½" brown rectangle to the right side of a unit from step 2. Press the seam allowances open.

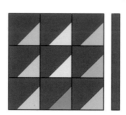

4. Sew a 1½" x 13½" brown rectangle to the bottom of the unit to complete the block. Press the seam allowances open. (The blue and green triangles should be floating in the brown background.) Repeat steps 3 and 4 to make a total of nine blocks.

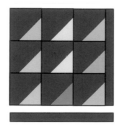

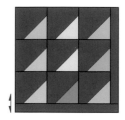

Make 9.

Quilt-Top Assembly

1. Referring to "Assembling the Quilt Top" on page 14, lay out the blocks in three rows of three blocks each, making sure to orient each block exactly as shown.

2. Sew the blocks together in rows, pressing the seam allowances open. Sew the rows together and press.

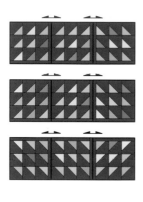

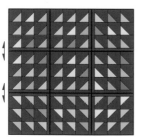

Finishing the Quilt

Refer to pages 15–24 for finishing your quilt, or take it to your favorite long-arm quilter for finishing. Using the 2¼"-wide brown tone-on-tone binding strips, make and attach binding.

In Formation

FINISHED QUILT: 45½" x 45½" | FINISHED BLOCK: 4½" x 9"

Materials

Yardage is based on 42"-wide fabric. Fat quarters measure 18" x 21".

2⅓ yards of off-white solid for background and binding

6 fat quarters of assorted light-peach to dark-tan solids for blocks

4 fat quarters of assorted light- to medium-green solids for blocks

3⅛ yards of fabric for backing

51" x 51" piece of batting

Cutting

From *each* of the 10 solid fat quarters, cut:

5 rectangles, 5" x 9½", using cutting diagram below (50 total)

From the off-white solid, cut:

13 strips, 5" x 42"; crosscut into 100 squares, 5" x 5"

5 binding strips, 2¼" x 42"

Use a gradation of solid colors in two complementary colorways to create this bold quilt.

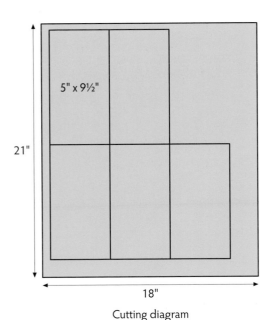

5" x 9½"

21"

18"

Cutting diagram

Pieced and machine quilted by Julie Herman

Making the Blocks

1. Draw a diagonal line on the wrong side of each off-white square. Place a marked square on one end of a solid-colored rectangle, right sides together, and sew along the marked line as shown. Trim away the corner fabric, leaving a ¼" seam allowance. Press the seam allowances open.

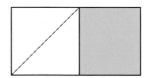
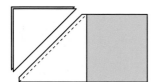

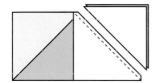

2. Place a second marked square on the opposite end of the rectangle, right sides together. Sew along the marked line and trim as before. Press the seam allowances open. Repeat steps 1 and 2 to make a total of 50 Flying Geese blocks.

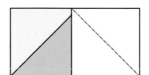
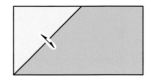

Quilt-Top Assembly

1. Referring to "Assembling the Quilt Top" on page 14, lay out the Flying Geese blocks in five vertical rows of 10 blocks each. Follow the diagram carefully to ensure proper color placement and to orient the blocks correctly. Sew the blocks into vertical rows; press the seam allowances open.

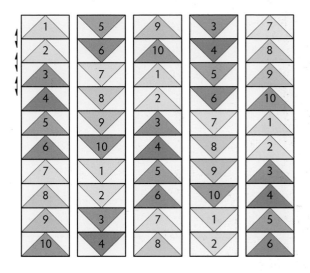

2. Sew the rows together and press the seam allowances open.

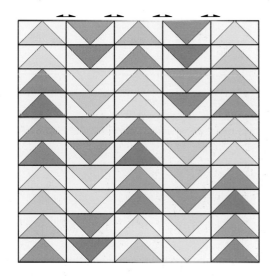

Finishing the Quilt

Refer to pages 15–24 for finishing your quilt, or take it to your favorite long-arm quilter for finishing. Using the 2¼"-wide off-white binding strips, make and attach binding.

Pieced by Julie Herman; machine quilted by Angela Walters

Dot Dot Dash

FINISHED QUILT: 48½" x 72½" | FINISHED BLOCK: 12" x 12"

Materials

Yardage is based on 42"-wide fabric.

50 strips, 2½" x 42", of assorted batiks for blocks
⅔ yard of gray batik for bias binding
¼ yard of yellow batik for binding flange
3⅓ yards of fabric for backing
54" x 78" piece of batting

Cutting

From 10 of the batik strips, cut *a total of:*
144 squares, 2½" x 2½"

From the remaining 40 batik strips, cut *a total of:*
120 rectangles, 2½" x 12½"

From the yellow batik, cut:
6 flange strips, ¾" x 42"

From the gray batik, cut:
255" of 2¼"-wide bias binding

Making the Blocks

1. Sew six different batik squares together to make a pieced strip. Press the seam allowances open. The strip should measure 12½" long. Repeat to make a total of 24 pieced strips.

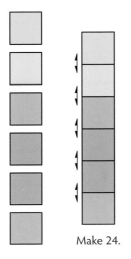

Make 24.

Precut strips make this quilt the perfect weekend project.

2. Lay out five different batik rectangles and one pieced strip as shown. Sew the pieces to complete the block. Repeat to make 24 blocks.

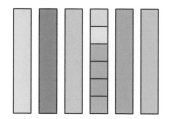 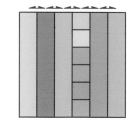

Make 24.

Quilt-Top Assembly

1. Referring to "Assembling the Quilt Top" on page 14, lay out the blocks in six rows of four blocks each, rotating every other block as shown below.
2. Sew the blocks in rows; press the seam allowances open. Sew the rows together and press.

Finishing the Quilt

Refer to pages 15–24 for finishing your quilt, or take it to your favorite long-arm quilter for finishing. Using the 3⁄4"-wide yellow batik strips, make and attach a binding flange. Using the 2 1⁄4"-wide bias binding strips, make and attach binding.

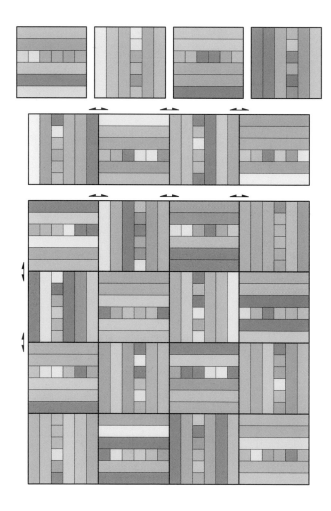

Boxed In

FINISHED QUILT: 51½" x 51½" | **FINISHED BLOCK:** 12" x 12"

Materials

Yardage is based on 42"-wide fabric.

1 yard of off-white print for blocks
⅞ yard of pink print for blocks
25 strips, 2½" x 42", of assorted prints for blocks
½ yard of light-colored striped fabric for binding
3½ yards of fabric for backing
57" x 57" piece of batting

Cutting

From the strips of assorted prints, cut:
384 squares, 2½" x 2½"

From the pink print, cut:
18 strips, 1½" x 42"; crosscut into:
    18 rectangles, 1½" x 12½"
    18 rectangles, 1½" x 10½"
    18 rectangles, 1½" x 6½"
    18 rectangles, 1½" x 4½"

From the off-white print, cut:
20 strips, 1½" x 42"; crosscut into:
    20 rectangles, 1½" x 12½"
    8 rectangles, 1½" x 11½"
    8 rectangles, 1½" x 10½"
    20 rectangles, 1½" x 6½"
    8 rectangles, 1½" x 5½"
    8 rectangles, 1½" x 4½"

From the light-colored striped fabric, cut:
6 binding strips, 2¼" x 42"

Set a dynamic block on point to create this show-stopping quilt.

Pieced by Julie Herman; machine quilted by Angela Walters

Making the Blocks

This is a one-block quilt. The illusion of a two-block quilt is created by fabric placement. Directions are included for making partial blocks to save fabric and time. However, if you prefer to make full blocks instead of partial blocks, additional fabric will be needed.

MAKING THE FULL BLOCKS

1. Lay out four different assorted squares in a four-patch arrangement as shown. Join the squares to complete the four-patch unit. Press the seam allowances open.

2. Sew 4½"-long pink rectangles to opposite sides of the four-patch unit. Press the seam allowances open. Then sew 6½"-long pink rectangles to the two remaining sides of the unit. Press the seam allowances open.

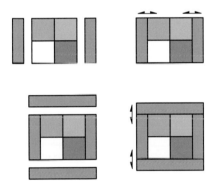

3. Select six different assorted squares. Join three squares to make a 6½"-long strip. Press the seam allowances open. Make two strips.

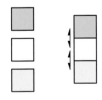

4. Sew the strips from step 3 to opposite sides of the unit from step 2. Press the seam allowances open.

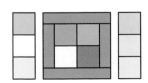
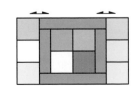

5. Select 10 different assorted squares. Join five squares to make a 10½"-long strip. Press the seam allowances open. Make two strips.

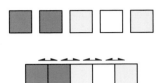

6. Sew the strips from step 5 to the unit from step 4 as shown. Press the seam allowances open.

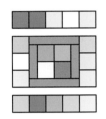
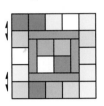

7. Sew 10½"-long pink rectangles to opposite sides of the unit from step 6. Press the seam allowances open. Then sew 12½"-long pink rectangles to the remaining two sides of the unit to complete the block. Press the seam allowances open. Repeat steps 1–7 to make a total of nine pink blocks.

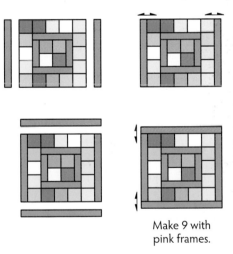

Make 9 with pink frames.

8. Repeat steps 1–7 using the off-white rectangles and assorted squares to make four off-white blocks.

Make 4 with off-white frames.

MAKING THE PARTIAL BLOCKS

1. Lay out three different assorted squares as shown. Join two squares and press the seam allowances open. Add the remaining square and press.

2. Sew a 5½"-long off-white rectangle to the left side of the unit from step 1. Press the seam allowances open. Sew a 6½"-long off-white rectangle to the top of the unit and press. The off-white strips will be longer than the unit.

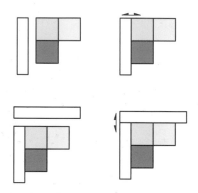

3. Select four different assorted squares. Join the squares to make an 8½"-long strip. Press the seam allowances open.

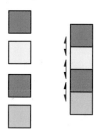

4. Sew the strip from step 3 to the left side of the unit from step 2. Press the seam allowances open.

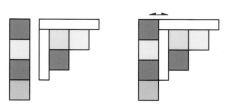

5. Select five different assorted squares. Join the squares to make a 10½"-long strip. Press the seam allowances open.

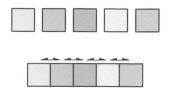

6. Sew the strip from step 5 to the top of the unit from step 4. Press the seam allowances open.

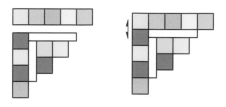

7. Sew an 11½"-long off-white rectangle to the left side of the unit from step 6. Press the seam allowances open. Sew a 12½"-long off-white rectangle to the top of the unit to complete a half block. Press the seam allowances open. Repeat steps 1–7 to make a total of eight partial blocks.

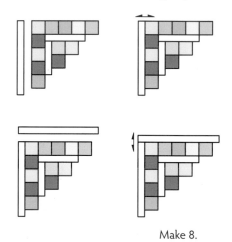

Make 8.

MAKING THE CORNER BLOCKS

1. Select seven different assorted squares. Join five squares to make a 10½"-long pieced strip. Join two squares to make a 4½"-long pieced strip. Press the seam allowances open.

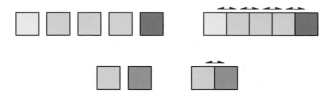

2. Arrange one 12½"-long off-white rectangle, the 10½"-long pieced strip, one 6½"-long off-white rectangle, and the 4½"-long pieced strip as shown. Fold each piece in half and finger-press to mark the center. Sew the pieces together, matching the center creases to make a corner block. Press the seam allowances open. Repeat to make a total of four corner blocks.

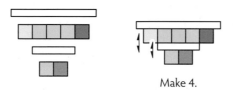

Make 4.

Quilt-Top Assembly

1. Referring to "Assembling the Quilt Top" on page 14, lay out the pink blocks, off-white blocks, partial blocks, and corner blocks in diagonal rows as shown. Sew the blocks together in rows, pressing the seam allowances open.

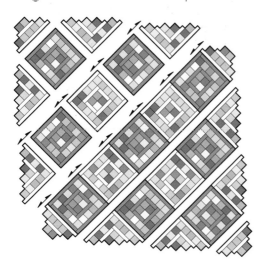

2. Sew the rows together and press. Trim and square up the quilt top, making sure to leave ¼" beyond the points of the blocks and squares for the seam allowance. Or, you can wait and trim the edges after the quilting is completed to avoid creating bias edges at this time.

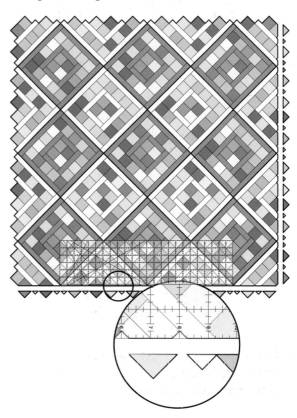

Finishing the Quilt

Refer to pages 15–24 for finishing your quilt, or take it to your favorite long-arm quilter for finishing. Using the 2¼"-wide light-colored striped binding strips, make and attach binding.

TWO-BLOCK QUILTS

Two-block quilts take advantage of using two different block designs in the layout, which sometimes creates a whole new and unexpected overall design. In some quilts, both blocks are pieced; in other quilts, one of the blocks is a plain square.

Square City

FINISHED QUILT: 67" x 67" | FINISHED BLOCK: 9½" x 9½"

This quilt is ideal for featuring large-scale prints in the blocks and plain squares.

Materials

Yardage is based on 42"-wide fabric. Fat quarters measure 18" x 21".

25 fat quarters of assorted prints for blocks
    and plain squares
1 yard of gray print for block centers
⅞ yard of large-scale striped fabric for bias binding
4⅜ yards of fabric for backing
73" x 73" piece of batting

Cutting

From the gray print, cut:
5 strips, 6" x 42"; crosscut 25 squares, 6" x 6"

From *each* of the 25 fat quarters, cut:
1 square, 10" x 10" (25 total; 1 is extra)
4 strips, 1½" x 18"; crosscut into:
    2 rectangles, 1½" x 10" (50 total)
    4 rectangles, 1½" x 8" (100 total)
    2 rectangles, 1½" x 6" (50 total)

From the large-scale striped fabric, cut:
280" of 2¼"-wide bias binding

Making the Blocks

1. Sew matching 1½" x 6" assorted rectangles to opposite sides of a gray square. Press the seam allowances open.

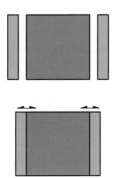

Pieced by Julie Herman; machine quilted by Angela Walters

2. Sew 1½" x 8" rectangles that match the rectangles in step 1 to the two remaining sides of the gray square. Press the seam allowances open.

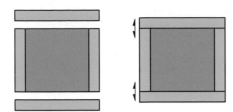

3. Sew matching 1½" x 8" assorted rectangles from a different print to opposite sides of the unit as shown. Press the seam allowances open.

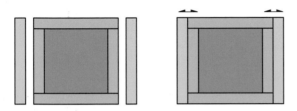

4. Sew 1½" x 10" rectangles that match the rectangles added in step 3 to the two remaining sides of the unit to complete the block. Press the seam allowances open. Repeat steps 1–4 to make a total of 25 blocks.

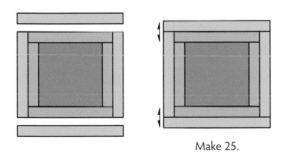

Make 25.

Quilt-Top Assembly

1. Referring to "Assembling the Quilt Top" on page 14, lay out the blocks and the 10" assorted squares in seven rows of seven units each, alternating the plain squares and the blocks in each row and from row to row.
2. Sew the blocks and squares together in rows; press the seam allowances open. Sew the rows together and press.

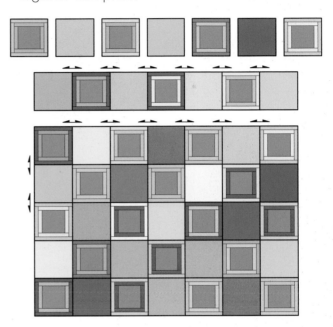

Finishing the Quilt

Refer to pages 15–24 for finishing your quilt, or take it to your favorite long-arm quilter for finishing. Using the 2¼"-wide bias binding strips, make and attach binding.

Pieced by Julie Herman; machine quilted by Angela Walters

Stars and Stripes

FINISHED QUILT: 44½" x 44½" | FINISHED BLOCK: 5½" x 5½"

Materials

*Yardage is based on 43"-wide (42"-wide) fabric.**

2¼ yards of white solid for blocks and bias binding
¼ yard of brown-and-blue zigzag print for blocks
⅛ (¼) yard of brown print for blocks
⅛ (¼) yard of brown-and-blue hexagon print for blocks
⅛ (¼) yard of blue print for blocks
⅛ (¼) yard of yellow print for blocks
⅛ (¼) yard of brown-and-yellow zigzag print for blocks
⅛ (¼) yard of orange print for blocks
⅛ (¼) yard of raspberry print for blocks
⅛ yard of green floral for blocks
⅛ yard of dark-green print for blocks
⅛ yard of light-green print for blocks
⅛ yard *each* of 4 assorted light prints for blocks
3 yards of fabric for backing
50" x 50" piece of batting
90° Double-Strip Ruler by Creative Grids (or other
   right-angle ruler with appropriate markings)

**See "Fabric Width" box, below right.*

Cutting

From the white solid, cut:
4 strips, 6" x 42"; crosscut into 20 squares, 6" x 6"
5 strips, 6¾" x 42"; crosscut into 22 squares,
   6¾" x 6¾". Cut the squares in half diagonally
   to yield 44 triangles.
190" of 2¼"-wide bias binding

From the brown-and-blue zigzag print, cut:
3 strips, 1½" x 42"

From the brown print, cut:
2 strips, 1½" x 42"

From the brown-and-blue hexagon print, cut:
2 strips, 1½" x 42"

From the blue print, cut:
2 strips, 1½" x 42"

Continued on page 56

Mix together striped blocks and solid squares to create the giant stars in this fun quilt.

FABRIC WIDTH

Typically, yardage and cutting calculations are based on 42"-wide fabric. But to make the most of using the 90° Double-Strip Ruler and your fabric, after trimming off the selvages, the fabric needs to measure at least 43" wide for this project. *OR*, if your fabric is narrower, you'll need the amount of fabric indicated in parentheses to cut all the required pieces for the project.

From the yellow print, cut:
2 strips, 1½" x 42"

From the brown-and-yellow zigzag print, cut:
2 strips, 1½" x 42"

From the orange print, cut:
2 strips, 1½" x 42"

From the raspberry print, cut:
2 strips, 1½" x 42"

From the green floral, cut:
1 strip, 1½" x 42"

From the dark-green print, cut:
1 strip, 1½" x 42"

From the light-green print, cut:
1 strip, 1½" x 42"

From *each* of the 4 assorted light prints, cut:
1 strip, 1½" x 42" (4 total)

Making the Blocks

1. Sew one brown strip, one brown-and-blue zigzag strip, one brown-and-blue hexagon strip, and one blue strip together along their long edges to make a strip set. Press the seam allowances open. The strip set should be 4½" wide; if it's not, adjust your seam allowances and remake the strip set. Make a total of two blue strip sets.

Make 2 blue strip sets.

2. Repeat step 1 using the yellow strips, the brown-and-yellow zigzag strips, the orange strips, and the raspberry strips to make two orange strip sets. Use the remaining brown-and-blue zigzag strip, the green floral strip, the dark-green strip, and the light-green strip to make one green strip set. Use the light strips to make one light strip set.

Make 2 orange strip sets.   Make 1 green strip set.

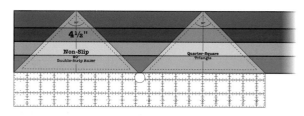

Make 1 light strip set.

3. Use the 90° Double-Strip Ruler to cut eight triangles from each strip set as shown. You'll need 16 blue triangles, 16 orange triangles, eight light triangles, and four green triangles. (If your strips are narrower than 43", you'll only be able to cut seven triangles from each strip set. Cut one strip from each fabric as needed to make one additional strip set in the required fabric combinations. Then cut triangles from the strip sets to achieve the desired number of triangles.)

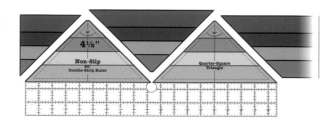

Cut 8 triangles from each strip set.

4. Pair a pieced triangle from step 3 with a white triangle and sew them along their long edges. Handle the pieced triangles carefully; the short sides are cut on the bias and can stretch out of shape. Press the seam allowances open. Trim the block to measure 6" square. Repeat to make a total of 44 blocks.

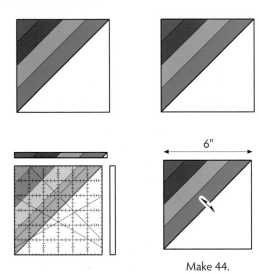

Make 44.

Quilt-Top Assembly

1. Referring to "Assembling the Quilt Top" on page 14, lay out the blocks and the white squares in eight rows of eight units each, being sure to orient the blocks as shown below.
2. Sew the blocks and squares together in rows; press the seam allowances in opposite directions from row to row. Sew the rows together and press.

Finishing the Quilt

Refer to pages 15–24 for finishing your quilt, or take it to your favorite long-arm quilter for finishing. Using the 2¼"-wide bias binding strips, make and attach binding.

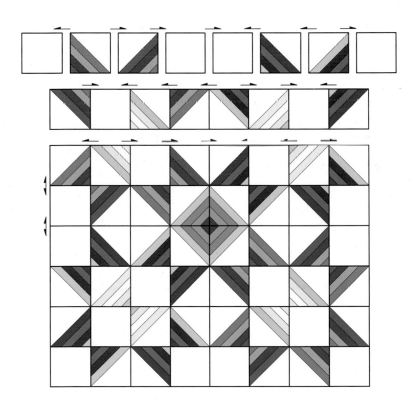

Pieced by Julie Herman; machine quilted by Angela Walters

Box of Chocolates

FINISHED QUILT: 64½" x 64½" | FINISHED BLOCK: 8" x 8"

Materials

*Yardage is based on 43"-wide (42"-wide) fabric.**

¼ (⅜) yard *each* of 32 assorted bright prints for blocks
⅝ yard of multicolored print for binding
4¼ yards of fabric for backing
70" x 70" piece of batting
90° Double-Strip Ruler by Creative Grids (or other right-angle ruler with appropriate markings)

See "Fabric Width" box, below right.

Cutting

From *each* of the 32 assorted bright prints, cut:
1 strip, 2" x 42" (32 total)
1 strip, 3" x 42" (32 total)

From multicolored print, cut:
7 binding strips, 2¼" x 42"

Making the Blocks

1. Using the assorted bright strips, sew a 2" strip to the long edge of a 3" strip to make a strip set. Choose the colors at random to achieve a scrappy design. Press the seam allowances open. The strip set should measure 4½" wide; if it doesn't, adjust your seam allowances and remake the strip set. Repeat to make a total of 32 strip sets.

Make 32 strip sets.

2. Use the 90° Double-Strip Ruler to cut eight triangles from each strip set as shown. You'll need four identical triangles for each block. (If your strips are narrower than 43" you'll only be able to cut seven triangles from each strip set. Cut one 2"-wide strip and one 3"-wide strip from each

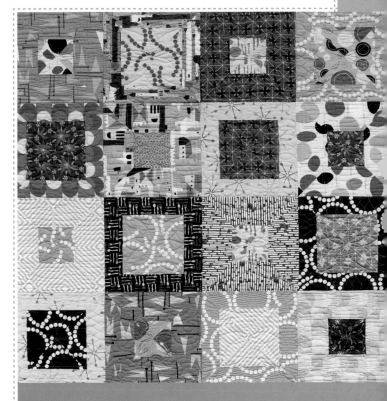

This quilt is created with strip sets. Sew them, cut them, and see what you end up with. You never know what you'll get, but a great quilt will be the result.

FABRIC WIDTH

Typically, yardage is based on 42"-wide fabric. But to make the most of using the 90° Double-Strip Ruler and your fabric, after trimming off the selvages, the fabric needs to measure at least 43" wide for this project. *OR*, if your fabric is narrower, you'll need the amount of fabric indicated in parentheses.

fabric as needed to make one additional strip set from like fabric combinations. Then cut triangles from the strip sets to achieve the required number of identical triangles.)

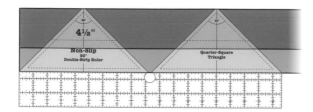

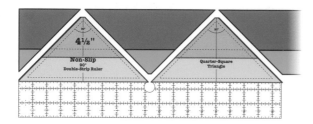

3. Arrange four identical triangles as shown. Sew the triangles in pairs, and then sew the pairs together to make a square. Handle the pieced triangles carefully; the short sides are cut on the bias and can stretch out of shape. Press the seam allowances open. Repeat to make a total of 32 blocks with a large center square and 32 blocks with a small center square.

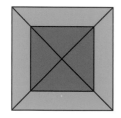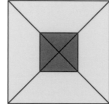

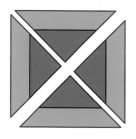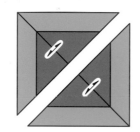

Make 32 of each.

Quilt-Top Assembly

1. Referring to "Assembling the Quilt Top" on page 14, lay out the blocks in eight rows of eight blocks each, alternating the large and small center squares in each row and from row to row as shown.
2. Sew the blocks together in rows, pressing the seam allowances open. Sew the rows together and press.

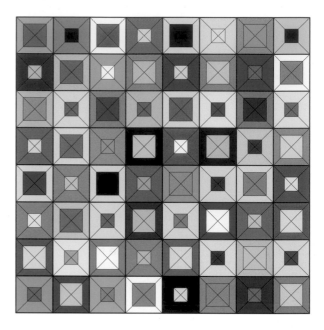

Finishing the Quilt

Refer to pages 15–24 for finishing your quilt, or take it to your favorite long-arm quilter for finishing. Using the 2¼"-wide multicolored binding strips, make and attach binding.

Raspberry Dessert

FINISHED QUILT: 77" x 77" | FINISHED BLOCK: 9" x 9"

Materials
Yardage is based on 42"-wide fabric.

3 yards of mauve tone-on-tone fabric for blocks
2⅝ yards of tan tone-on-tone fabric for blocks
    and binding
2 yards of bright-pink tone-on-tone fabric for blocks
1 yard of red tone-on-tone fabric for blocks
5 yards of fabric for backing
83" x 83" piece of batting

Cutting
From the red tone-on-tone fabric, cut:
8 strips, 3½" x 42"; crosscut into 84 squares,
    3½" x 3½"

From the bright-pink tone-on-tone fabric, cut:
32 strips, 2" x 42"; crosscut into:
    84 rectangles, 2" x 6½"
    42 rectangles, 2" x 5"
    126 rectangles, 2" x 3½"

From the mauve tone-on-tone fabric, cut:
48 strips, 2" x 42"; crosscut into:
    84 rectangles, 2" x 9½"
    126 rectangles, 2" x 6½"
    42 rectangles, 2" x 5"

From the tan tone-on-tone fabric, cut:
18 strips, 3½" x 42"; crosscut into:
    42 rectangles, 3½" x 9½"
    42 rectangles, 3½" x 6½"
9 binding strips, 2¼" x 42"

Two simple small blocks are combined, and then set
on point to create large diamonds in this luscious quilt.

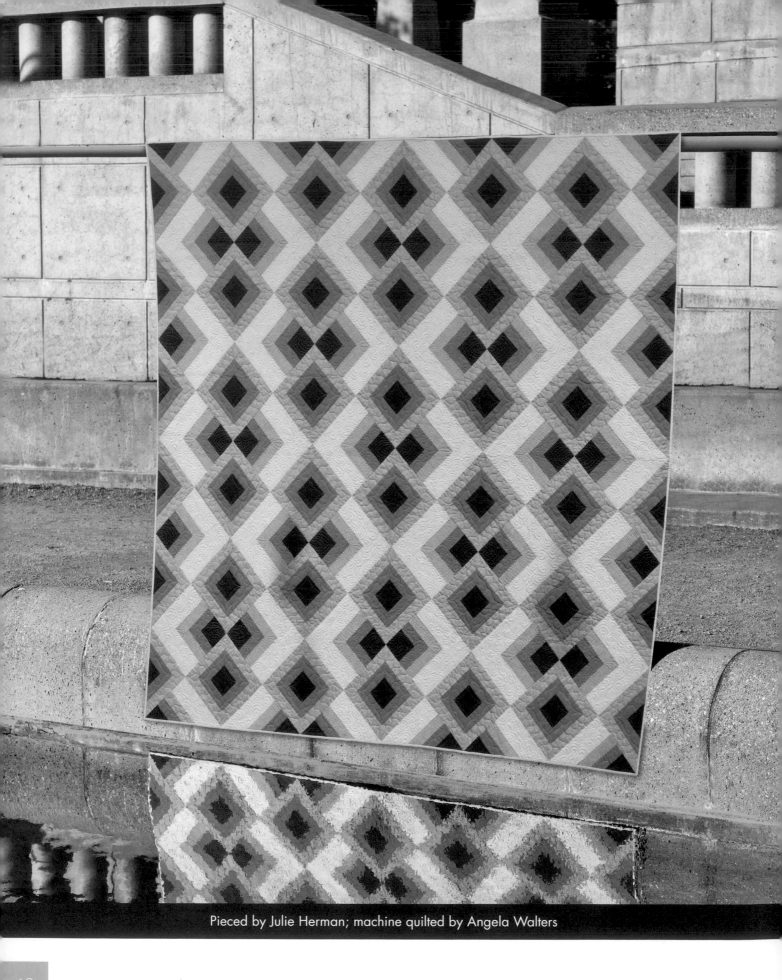

Pieced by Julie Herman; machine quilted by Angela Walters

Making Block A

1. Sew a 2" x 3½" bright-pink rectangle to the top of a 3½" red square. Press the seam allowances open. Sew a 2" x 5" bright-pink rectangle to the right side of the unit and press the seam allowances open.

2. Sew a 2" x 5" mauve rectangle to the top of the unit from step 1. Press the seam allowances open. Sew a 2" x 6½" mauve rectangle to the right side of the unit and press the seam allowances open.

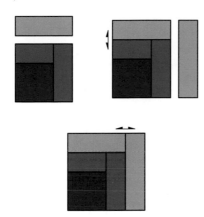

3. Sew a 3½" x 6½" tan rectangle to the top of the unit from step 2. Press the seam allowances open. Sew a 3½" x 9½" tan rectangle to the right side of the unit to complete the block. Press the seam allowances open. Repeat steps 1–3 to make a total of 42 blocks.

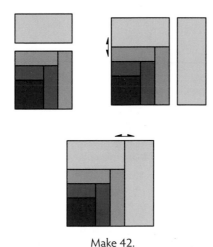

Make 42.

Making Block B

1. Sew 2" x 3½" bright-pink rectangles to opposite sides of a 3½" red square. Press the seam allowances open.

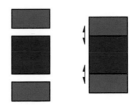

2. Sew 2" x 6½" bright-pink rectangles to the two remaining sides of the unit from step 1. Press the seam allowances open.

3. Sew 2" x 6½" mauve rectangles to the top and bottom of the unit from step 2. Press the seam allowances open.

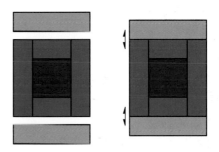

4. Sew 2" x 9½" mauve rectangles to the two remaining sides of the unit from step 3 to complete the block. Press the seam allowances open. Repeat steps 1–4 to make a total of 42 blocks.

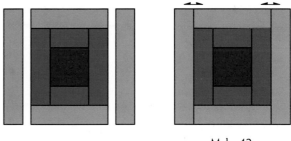

Make 42.

Quilt-Top Assembly

1. Referring to "Assembling the Quilt Top" on page 14, lay out the A and B blocks in diagonal rows, alternating them as shown at right, in each row and from row to row. Notice that the A blocks are rotated so that the tan rectangles form vertical zigzag lines. Sew the blocks together in rows, pressing the seam allowances open.
2. Sew the rows together and press. Trim and square up the quilt top, making sure to leave ¼" beyond the points of the blocks for seam allowances as shown below. Or, you can wait and trim the edges after the quilting is completed to avoid creating bias edges at this time.

Finishing the Quilt

Refer to pages 15–24 for finishing your quilt, or take it to your favorite long-arm quilter for finishing. Using the 2¼"-wide tan binding strips, make and attach binding.

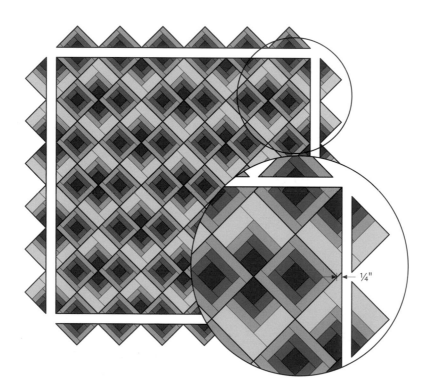

¼"

OUTSIDE-THE-BLOCK QUILTS

Instead of conventional square blocks, the quilt designs in this section are based on row quilts (both horizontal and vertical), rectangular shapes, and layouts that don't have a recognizable block. Step outside the block to create these unique quilts.

Pieced by Julie Herman; machine quilted by Angela Walters

Rows of Bricks

FINISHED QUILT: 57½" X 75½"

Materials

Yardage is based on 42"-wide fabric.

¼ yard *each* of 19 assorted bright prints for horizontal rows

1⅞ yards of gray print for horizontal bars and binding

5 yards of fabric for backing*

63" x 81" piece of batting

*If your fabric measures a true 42" wide after trimming off the selvages, you'll only need 3⅞ yards of fabric for backing.

Cutting

From *each* of 8 assorted bright prints, cut:

1 strip, 5" x 42"; crosscut into:

    3 rectangles, 5" x 10" (24 total)

    1 rectangle, 5" x 5¼" (8 total)

From *each* of the remaining 11 assorted bright prints, cut:

1 strip, 5" x 42"; crosscut into 4 rectangles, 5" x 10" (44 total)

From the *lengthwise grain* of the gray print, cut:

3 strips, 7½" x 57½"

5 binding strips, 2¼" x 57"

Making the Rows

1. Sew six different 5" x 10" assorted rectangles end to end to make a row. Press the seam allowances open. Make eight rows.

This quilt is ideal for large-scale, stunning prints that need a place to shine.

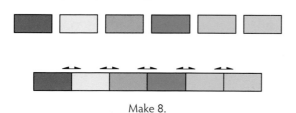

Make 8.

2. Sew five different 5" x 10" assorted rectangles end to end to make a row. Sew a 5" x 5¼" assorted rectangle to each end to complete the row. Press the seam allowances open. Make four of these rows.

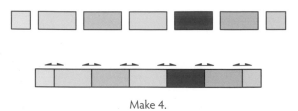

Make 4.

3. Sew a row from step 1 to each long side of a row from step 2 to complete a pieced section. Press the seam allowances open. Make four pieced sections.

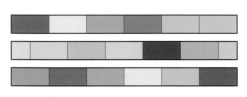

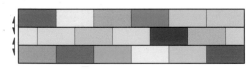

Make 4.

Quilt-Top Assembly

1. Referring to "Assembling the Quilt Top" on page 14, lay out the four pieced sections and the 7½"-wide gray strips, alternating them as shown.

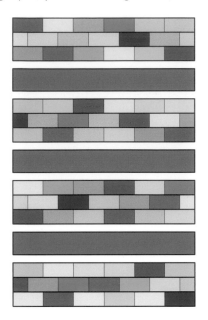

2. Sew the sections and strips together to complete the quilt top. Press the seam allowances open.

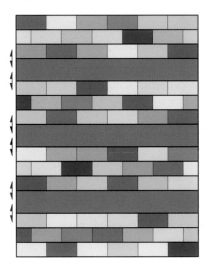

Finishing the Quilt

Refer to pages 15–24 for finishing your quilt, or take it to your favorite long-arm quilter for finishing. Using the 2¼"-wide gray binding strips, make and attach binding.

Framed Coins

FINISHED QUILT: 72½" x 72½" | FINISHED BLOCK: 12" x 24"

Materials

Yardage is based on 42"-wide fabric.

⅛ yard *each* of 36 assorted black-and-white prints for blocks

⅞ yard of apple-green solid for blocks

⅞ yard of kiwi-green solid for blocks

⅔ yard of clover-green solid for blocks

⅔ yard of willow-green solid for blocks

⅞ yard of black-and-white dotted fabric for bias binding

4⅞ yards of fabric for backing

79" x 79" piece of batting

Cutting

From *each* of the 36 assorted black-and-white prints, cut:

1 strip, 3" x 42"; crosscut into 4 rectangles, 3" x 8½" (144 total)

From the apple-green solid, cut:

10 strips, 2½" x 42"; crosscut into:
    10 rectangles, 2½" x 20½"
    10 rectangles, 2½" x 12½"

From the kiwi-green solid, cut:

10 strips, 2½" x 42"; crosscut into:
    10 rectangles, 2½" x 20½"
    10 rectangles, 2½" x 12½"

From the clover-green solid, cut:

8 strips, 2½" x 42"; crosscut into:
    8 rectangles, 2½" x 20½"
    8 rectangles, 2½" x 12½"

From the willow-green solid, cut:

8 strips, 2½" x 42"; crosscut into:
    8 rectangles, 2½" x 20½"
    8 rectangles, 2½" x 12½"

From the black-and-white dotted fabric, cut:

300" of 2¼"-wide bias binding

Combine rectangular blocks and a fun setting to create this dynamic quilt.

Pieced by Julie Herman; machine quilted by Angela Walters

Making the Blocks

1. Sew eight different black-and-white rectangles along their long sides to form a strip. Press the seam allowances open. The strip should measure 8½" x 20½".

2. Sew matching 2½" x 20½" green rectangles to the long sides of the black-and-white strip. Press the seam allowances open.

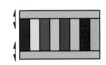

3. Sew 2½" x 12½" green rectangles that match the rectangles in step 2 to the short sides of the strip unit to complete the block. Press the seam allowances open. The block should measure 12½" x 20½". Repeat steps 1–3 to make a total of 18 blocks.

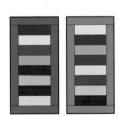

Make 18.

Unit Assembly

1. Sew a clover-green block to the long side of a willow-green block. Press the seam allowances open. Repeat to make four of these units.

Make 4.

2. Sew a kiwi-green block to the bottom of a unit from step 1 to complete the top-right section of the quilt top. Press the seam allowances open.

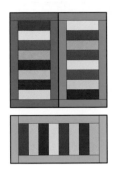 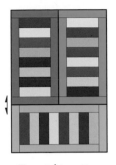

Top-right section

3. Sew an apple-green block to the top of a unit from step 1 to complete the bottom-left section of the quilt top. Press the seam allowances open.

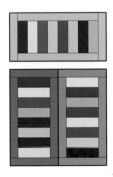 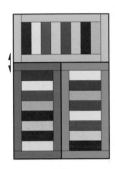

Bottom-left section

4. Sew a kiwi-green block to the left side and an apple-green block to the right side of a unit from step 1. Press the seam allowances open. Make two units.

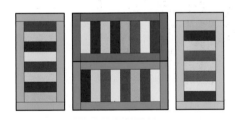

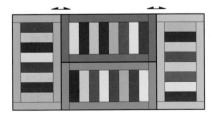

Make 2.

5. Sew an apple-green block and a kiwi-green block together along their short sides. Press the seam allowances open. Make two units.

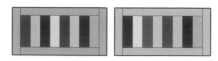

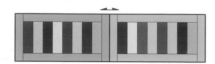

Make 2.

6. Sew a unit from step 5 to the top of a unit from step 4 to complete the top-left section. Press the seam allowances open.

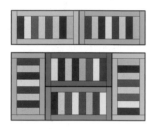 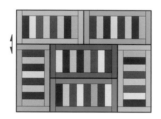

Top-left section

7. Sew a unit from step 5 to the bottom of a unit from step 4 to complete the bottom-right section. Press the seam allowances open.

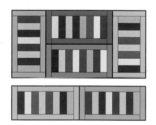 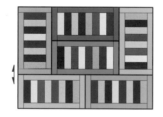

Bottom-right section

Quilt-Top Assembly

1. Referring to "Assembling the Quilt Top" on page 14, lay out the four sections.
2. Sew the sections together in rows. Press the seam allowances open. Sew the rows together and press the seam allowances open.

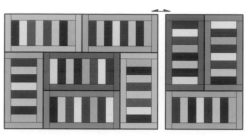

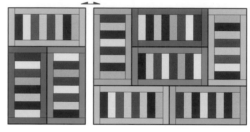

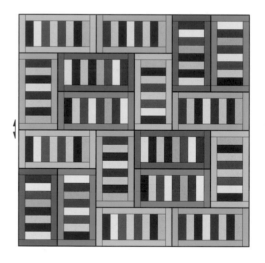

Finishing the Quilt

Refer to pages 15–24 for finishing your quilt, or take it to your favorite long-arm quilter for finishing. Using the 2¼"-wide bias binding strips, make and attach binding.

In Between

FINISHED QUILT: 44¼" x 50" | **FINISHED BLOCK:** 7" x 7"

Materials

Yardage is based on 42"-wide fabric.

⅞ yard of yellow floral for vertical sashing rows
⅝ yard of purple-floral batik for setting triangles
⅝ yard of dark-purple batik for setting triangles
⅜ yard of purple batik for blocks
⅓ yard *each* of 2 light-purple prints for blocks
⅔ yard of yellow print for bias binding
3 yards of fabric for backing
50" x 56" piece of batting

Cutting

From *each* of the 2 light-purple prints, cut:
3 strips, 2½" x 42" (6 total)

From the purple batik, cut:
3 strips, 3½" x 42"

From the purple-floral batik, cut:
1 strip, 11½" x 42"; crosscut into 3 squares,
    11½" x 11½". Cut the squares into quarters
    diagonally to yield 12 triangles.
1 strip, 6" x 42"; crosscut into 3 squares, 6" x 6".
    Cut the squares in half diagonally to yield 6
    triangles.

From the dark-purple batik, cut:
1 strip, 11½" x 42"; crosscut into 3 squares,
    11½" x 11½". Cut the squares into quarters
    diagonally to yield 12 triangles.
1 strip, 6" x 42"; crosscut into 3 squares, 6" x 6".
    Cut the squares in half diagonally to yield 6
    triangles.

From the yellow floral, cut:
6 strips, 4" x 42"

From the yellow print, cut:
200" of 2¼"-wide bias binding

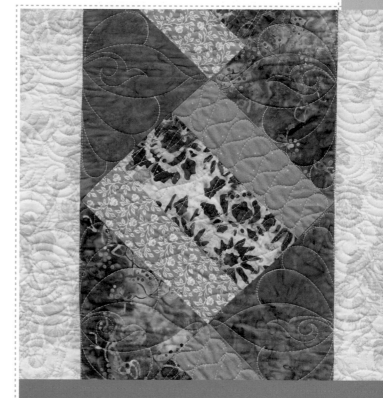

Set simple blocks on point for a bold design.

Pieced by Julie Herman; machine quilted by Angela Walters

Making the Vertical Rows

1. Sew a light-purple strip to one long side of a purple batik strip. Sew a different light-purple strip to the other long side of the purple batik strip to make a strip set. Press the seam allowances open. Repeat to make a total of three strip sets. Cut the strip sets into 15 blocks, 7½" wide.

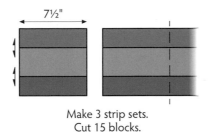

7½"

Make 3 strip sets.
Cut 15 blocks.

2. Arrange five blocks, eight quarter-square triangles, and four half-square triangles, alternating the purple-floral and dark-purple triangles as shown. Sew the triangles to opposite sides of each block and press the seam allowances open.

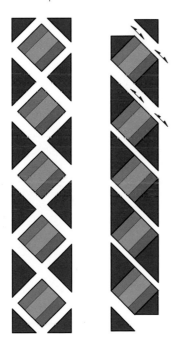

3. Sew the units together and add the remaining two half-square triangles to complete a vertical row. The row should measure 50" long. Repeat to make a total of three rows.

Make 3.

Quilt-Top Assembly

1. Sew the yellow-floral strips end to end to make a long strip. From the strip, cut four 50"-long strips.
2. Referring to "Assembling the Quilt Top" on page 14, lay out the block rows and yellow strips, alternating them as shown. Sew the rows and strips together; press the seam allowances open.

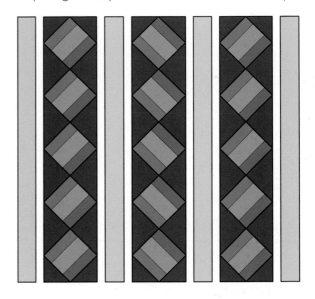

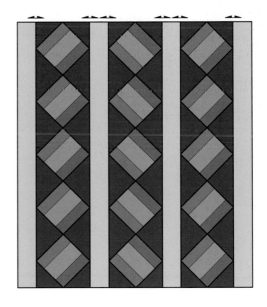

Finishing the Quilt

Refer to pages 15–24 for finishing your quilt, or take it to your favorite long-arm quilter for finishing. Using the 2¼"-wide bias binding strips, make and attach binding.

Pieced by Julie Herman; machine quilted by Angela Walters

Checkerboard Dots

FINISHED QUILT: 48½" x 48½"

Materials

Yardage is based on 42"-wide fabric.
Fat quarters measure 18" x 21".

32 fat quarters of assorted batiks for backgrounds
   and circle appliqués
⅛ yard *each* of 6 assorted batiks for scrappy
   bias binding
3¼ yards of fabric for backing
54" x 54" piece of batting
2¾ yards of 16"-wide fusible web

Cutting

**From the 32 fat quarters of assorted batiks,
cut a *total of*:**
16 squares, 9½" x 9½"
16 rectangles, 6½" x 9½"
4 squares, 6½" x 6½"

Set aside remaining fabric for appliqué circles.

From *each* ⅛-yard cut of an assorted batik, cut:
1 binding strip, 2¼" x 42" (6 total)

Making the Quilt

This design is scrappy, so don't overplan.

1. Lay out the 9½" batik squares, 6½" batik squares,
   and batik rectangles in six rows as shown.

Showcase large-scale prints in this striking quilt.

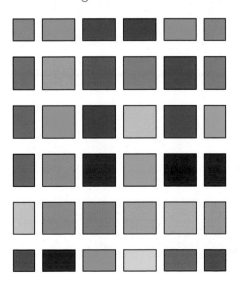

2. Sew the pieces together into rows. Press the seam allowances open. Sew the rows together and press.

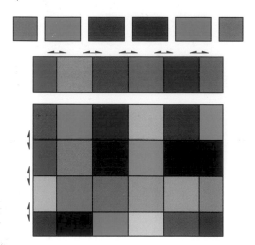

3. Using the pattern below, trace 25 circles onto the paper side of the fusible web. Roughly cut out the circles, approximately ¼" outside the traced line. Fuse each circle to the wrong side of a different batik. Cut out each circle directly on the traced line.

4. Remove the paper backing and fuse the circles in place, centering them on top of the seam intersections as shown. Stitch the circles in place using a machine blanket stitch or a zigzag stitch.

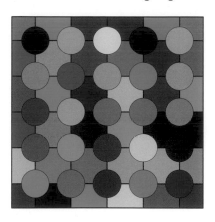

Finishing the Quilt

Refer to pages 15–24 for finishing your quilt, or take it to your favorite long-arm quilter for finishing. Using the 2¼"-wide batik strips, make and attach scrappy bias binding. Refer to "Making Scrappy Bias Binding" on page 24 as needed.

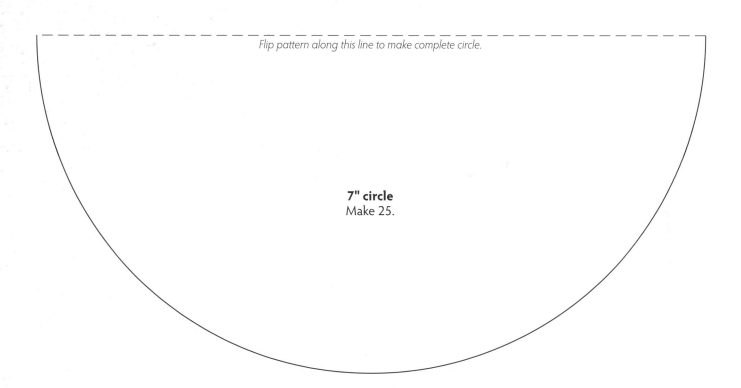

Flip pattern along this line to make complete circle.

7" circle
Make 25.

Acknowledgments

- Angela Walters, for her amazing quilting throughout the book.

- Allison Benjamin, for believing in me before anyone else outside my family did. Without her encouragement and friendship, I wouldn't be where I am today.

- Rachael Pannepacker, for her wise words: "If writing a book was easy, everyone would do it."

- Tricia Landes and Candi Weinrick, for their countless hours of sewing, testing, reading, editing, support, and friendship. You two are the best.

- Lawrence Kaplan, for his love, support, and patience, and for editing my book.

- Thank you to Natalie Barnes, Liz Cairo, Susan DiBartolo, Rachel Griffith, Joan Hawley, Allie Heath, Lizzy House, Jessica Levitt, Maryann Scanlon, and the entire Philadelphia Modern Quilt Guild for support and guidance.

- Thank you to the following fabric companies for providing beautiful fabric for this book: Robert Kaufman, Michael Miller, Freespirit, and Moda. Thank you to The Warm Company for providing all the batting.

- Thank you to the amazing team at Martingale: Karen Soltys and Cathy Reitan, for their support and guidance. Nancy Mahoney and Sheila Ryan, for the fantastic editing. Paula Schlosser and Adrienne Smitke, for designing a beautiful layout and feel for this book. Brent Kane, for listening to my vision and photographing my quilts in a way that fit my style.

- Last but not least, thank you to the readers of Jaybird Quilts. Your support, comments, photos, and blog posts inspire me. You are why I wrote this book. Make quilts that make you happy.

About the Author

photo by Brad Herman

JULIE HERMAN is better known in the quilting community as *Jaybird*. So where did the name come from? A childhood nickname, of course! Jaybird is short for Julie-Bird, and Julie can't remember a time before her brother gave her the nickname. It stuck within the family, but it wasn't until she decided to name her blog Jaybird Quilts that other people started calling her Jaybird.

Her sewing journey began in the summer of 2002 when she "borrowed" her mom's sewing machine. She never actually gave that machine back and sewed over 200 quilts on it before getting a new machine.

Julie is a self-taught quilter and designer with a Bachelor of Science degree in Visual Studies and Design from Drexel University in Philadelphia, Pennsylvania. Completing her Master's degree in Education, also at Drexel, prepared her to teach quilting classes. Julie loves the "I get it!" moment her students experience when they learn a new technique.

Julie recently moved across the country from the East Coast to the West Coast and now is happy to have her entire family together. Before moving, Julie founded the Philadelphia chapter of the Modern Quilt Guild.

An active blogger, Julie has had her quilts published in numerous quilting magazines. She has a quilt-pattern line, also called Jaybird Quilts. Keep up with Julie's latest quilting adventures on her website, jaybirdquilts.com, where you can read her blog, learn about her quilting inspirations, and find out where you can purchase her quilt patterns. Her motto is, "One girl on a mission to make life better with fabric!"